# mustsees SINGAPORE

Lion statue, Haw Par Villa/J. Gilbert/Michelin

MICHELIN

| | |
|---|---|
| **General Manager** | Cynthia Clayton Ochterbeck |

**must**sees Singapore

| | |
|---|---|
| **Editor** | Jonathan P. Gilbert |
| **Contributing Writers** | Gwen Cannon, Emma Levine, John Malathronas, Adrian Mourby, Neil Ray, Zijia Wong, Daven Wu |
| **Production Manager** | Natasha G. George |
| **Cartography** | GeoNova Publishing Inc., Apa Publications |
| **Photo Editor** | Yoshimi Kanazawa |
| **Researcher** | Sean Cannon |
| **Proofreaders** | Claiborne Linvill |
| **Layout** | Nicole D. Jordan |
| **Cover & Interior Design** | Chris Bell |

**Contact Us**

Michelin Maps and Guides
One Parkway South
Greenville, SC 29615
USA
www.michelintravel.com

Michelin Maps and Guides
Hannay House
39 Clarendon Road
Watford, Herts WD17 1JA
UK
☎(01923) 205 240
www.ViaMichelin.com
travelpubsales@uk.michelin.com

**Special Sales**

For information regarding bulk sales, customized editions and premium sales, please contact our Customer Service Departments:

| | |
|---|---|
| USA | 1-800-432-6277 |
| UK | (01923) 205 240 |
| Canada | 1-800-361-8236 |

**Michelin Apa Publications Ltd**

**A joint venture between Michelin and Langenscheidt**

58 Borough High Street, London SE1 1XF, United Kingdom


ISBN 978-1-906261-97-9
Printed: April 2010
Printed and bound: Himmer Winco, China

**Note to the reader:**
While every effort is made to ensure that all information printed in this guide is correct and up-to-date, Michelin Apa Publications Ltd. accepts no liability for any direct, indirect or consequential losses howsoever caused so far as such can be excluded by law. Admission prices listed for sights in this guide are for a single adult, unless otherwise specified.

# Welcome to Singapore



Vesak celebrations in Chinatown

TABLE OF CONTENTS

p 66

J. Gilbert/Michelin

## Introduction



## Must See

p 88

J. Gilbert/Michelin

p104
J. Gilbert/Michelin

p 104
J. Gilbert/Michelin



## Must Do

p 110
J. Gilbert/Michelin

## Must Eat



## Must Stay



## Must Know

# ★★★ ATTRACTIONS

Unmissable historic, cultural and natural sights

Night Safari p 85

Raffles Hotel p 54

Singapore Botanic Gardens p 84

National Orchid Garden p 84

J. Gilbert/Michelin

"Songs of the Sea" water-pyrotechnics show p 97

J. Gilbert/Michelin

Siloso Beach p 96

Singapore Zoological Gardens p 98

# ACTIVITIES

Unmissable activities and entertainment

Watching Dragon Boat Races p 91

Cycling on Pulau Ubin p 90

Tai Chi at East Coast Park p 99

Sentosa Golf Club p 90

J. Gilbert/Michelin

Relaxing on Sentosa's beach p 94

© Singapore Tourism Board

Riding the Sentosa Luge p 97

J. Gilbert/Michelin

Kayaking on MacRitchie Reservoir p 87

J. Gilbert/Michelin

Shopping in Little India p 107

# ★★★ ATTRACTIONS

**Unmissable historic, cultural and natural sights**

For more than 75 years people have used Michelin stars to take the guesswork out of travel. Our star-rating system helps you make the best decision on where to go, what to do, and what to see.

| | |
|---|---|
| ★★★ | Unmissable |
| ★★ | Worth a trip |
| ★ | Worth a detour |
| **No star** | Recommended |

## ★★★Three Star



## ★★Two Star



## ★One Star

**Unmissable activities, entertainment, restaurants and hotels**

For every historic and natural sight in Singapore there are a thousand more activities. We recommend all of the activities in this guide, but our top picks are highlighted with the Michelin Man logo.

### Outings

Day at the zoo *p 98*
Ride the river *p 49*
Hippo bus tour *p 14*
Explore a reserve *p 84*
Island hop *p 17*
Admire artefacts *p 78*
View Harry Potter stamps *p 82*
See forever at Sky Tower *p 95*
Get friendly with insects *p 95*
Walk over treetops *p 87*
Ride a trishaw *p 30*
Tan at Tanjong Beach *p 91*
See Buddha's tooth *p 42*

### Hotels

Berjaya Hotel *p 145*
The Fullerton *p 148*
Gallery Hotel *p 150*
Goodwood Park *p 77, p 152*
New Majestic *p 147*
Raffles Hotel *p 54, p 148*
The Scarlet *p 145*
Sentosa Resort *p 155*
Sleepy Sam's *p 151*
Strand *p 147*

### Nightlife

Get wild at Night Safari *p 85*
Watch Chinese Opera *p 101*
Enter the Esplanade *p 101*
Drama at W!ld Rice *p 102*
Bar hop at Chijmes *p 114*
Tapas out at Cuba Libre *p 115*
Stay til dawn at Balcony Bar *p 114*
Cheap beer at Cuscaden *p 115*
Wining at Tasting Notes *p 119*
DJ nights at Zirca *p 119*
Sunday jams at Crazy Elephant *p 120*
Join the crowds at Harry's *p 120*
Stock up at Chinatown Night Market *p 105*

### Relax

Drink a cool beverage at Alley Bar *p 76*
Wander among orchids *p 86*
Try reflexology *p 122*
Sip a Singapore Sling *p 118*
Have a Balinese massage *p 122*

### Restaurants

Banana Leaf Apolo p *137*
BLU, for the view *p 143*
The Blue Ginger *p 128*
Café Iguana for Tex Mex *p 129*
Lei Garden's dim sum *p 132*
Food Republic *p 138*
Jade *p 131*
Les Amis *p 142*
Li Bai for Cantonese *p 143*
Majestic for modern Chinese cuisine *p 130*
Mezza9's brunch *p 141*
Newton Food Centre *p 143*
North Indian fare at Muthu's Curry *p 138*
Yhingthai Palace *p 132*

### Shopping

Discounts *p 105, p 113*
Chinese herbs *p 39*
Tekka Market *p 59*
Indonesian batik *p 109*
Jade carvings *p 106*
Vintage jewellery *p 110*
Raffles arcade *p 106*
Mall heaven *p 111*
Gadget heaven *p 50*
Arab Street's textile shops *p 109*
Urban wear *p 106, 109*
Books galore *p 105, p 112*
All things silk *p 107*
Indian clothing *p 109*
Fleamarket *p 108*

### Sports

Bike the island *p 90*
Fomula 1 action *p 93*
Scuba dive *p 90*
See a polo match *p 92*
Swim and sunbathe *p 91*
Swing a club *p 90*
Watch cricket *p 91*
Windsurf *p 91*

MUST KNOW

# IDEAS AND TOURS

Throughout this thematic guide you will find inspiration for a thousand different holidays in Singapore. The following is a selection of ideas to start you off. The sites in **bold** are found in the Index.

## WALKING TOURS

Singapore is a great (and incredibly safe) place to wander around, be it the malls, the riverbanks or the tropical gardens.

*The following self-guided walking tours feature in DISTRICTS:*

### Chinatown★★

Recent heritage projects have ensured that Chinatown retains its unmistakable ethnic character, especially along the five roads that run from Pagoda Street to **Sago Street★**. This district is a place to shop, eat and celebrate the financial and cultural contribution that generations of Chinese have made to Singapore.

### Central Business District★

Singapore's business district is a shiny cityscape of huge high rises and extraordinary affluence. On a more human scale, the CBD also takes in **Boat Quay★★**—a collection of shophouses huddled at the feet of towering skyscrapers where financiers go to play at the end of the day—and older buildings like the **Fullerton Building★★** and **Clifford Pier** that recall the colonial past.

### Colonial District★★

#### Fort Canning★★

This walk starts on Singapore's tall, fortified hill and combines pre-colonial history and World War II monuments with modern city landmarks. From the Tombs of the Kings of Ancient Singapura and **Malaya Command Headquarters** of World War II to **Clarke Quay★★**, the centre of Singapore's nightlife, this walk encapsulates in a few hours six centuries of history.

#### The Padang★★

An easy stroll of the area around the historic **Padang★** sports field on the north side of the Singapore river allows you to discover the

*Boat Quay and the skyscrapers of the CBD*

J. Gilbert/Michelin

city's strong colonial heritage. From the **Old Assembly House★** (now the **Arts House★**), the first building to be erected by the British, to the **Old Supreme Court★★**, which was the last, this walk takes in some of Southeast Asia's best colonial architecture.

### Raffles and the Marina★★

**Raffles Hotel★★★**, the **Singapore Flyer★★**, Suntec City's **Fountain of Wealth★**, the **Singapore Art Museum** and the **Cathedral of the Good Shepherd★** are some of the many sights in this tour that blend interesting glimpses of the 19C settlement with the latest attractions of the new, global city.

## Little India★★

A veritable assault on the senses as the traditional East finally reveals itself exultantly alongside the contemporary Western façade of modern Singapore. You can shop here 24/7 at the **Mustafa Centre★**, have a meal served on a banana leaf in a south Indian restaurant or browse the stalls in the covered markets. Above all, you will see some spectacular Indian and Buddhist temples and a beautifully decorated mosque.

## Kampong Glam and the Arab Quarter★★

A visit to the Muslim neighbourhood includes Singapore's first palace, picturesque mosques and traditional, small shops situated in quaint, narrow lanes. Marvel at the golden domes of the **Sultan Mosque★★**, admire artefacts and gardens at the **Malay Heritage Centre★**, and see a minaret called the "Leaning Tower of Singapore".

*Orchids in the Singapore Botanic Gardens*



## Orchard Road Area

### Singapore Botanic Gardens★★★

More than 150 years old, these gardens show off flora, rain forest and an astounding collection of orchids. They also reveal the origins of Singapore's national symbol, and the reasons orchid hybridisation became such a success.

### Dhoby Ghaut Area

This area showcases Singapore's multicultural identity, with places of worship for Christians, Hindus, Confucians and Jews, plus wealthy Chinese clans. En route via a skate park, the walk ends at the famous Peranakan houses of **Emerald Hill★**.

### Scotts Road Area

Some of Singapore's finest colonial houses cluster around Scotts Road, with characteristic black-and-white **bungalows** built for the city's civil servants in the early 19C. After circling Goodwood Crescent, the walk ends at the century-old **Goodwood Park Hotel**, built in a style evoking the fairytale castles that overlook the Rhine River in Germany.

## GUIDED TOURS

### Guided Walks

If you prefer to be shown around by a resident, you can simply turn up at one of the departure points for the **Original Singapore Walks®** (*S$25–40, S$15 children; 6325 1631; www.singaporewalks.com*) for an impromptu tour. The guides come from various backgrounds and include actors, authors, and authorities on the subject of the walks, from the adult-only **"Secrets of the Red Lantern"** tour to the **"Sultans of Spice"** tour in Kampong Glam (*see DISTRICTS*).

### River Tours

The river has always played an important role in the lives of Singaporeans. At one time it looked as though the old quayside houses were to be bulldozed into oblivion as banks, multinationals and the like sought to transform Singapore into a modern wonderland. Thankfully, someone realised the potential of keeping the old shophouses and warehouses, and like many dockland developments across the world, Singapore now has some trendy waterfront venues in the shape of smart cafés and night spots. Once working wharves where local labourers unloaded ships from the west and the east, now **Clarke Quay★★** and **Boat Quay★★** are inviting places to relax, sip a cool drink and watch the river activities.

At the mouth of the river stands the famous **Merlion★**, half fish and half lion, a seemingly ancient structure that was placed in its present location as recently as 1972. Operated by Singapore River Cruises, river trips run from Clarke Quay to **Clifford Pier**; a longer 45-minute trip goes from **Boat Quay** to **Roberton Quay** and back. An alternative is to take the river taxi, or the amphibious **DUCKtours** (*S$33, S$17 children; 6338 6877; www.ducktours.com.sg*). Although only 4km/2.5mi long, the river offers an interesting view of the city as a commercial and historical centre.

**Singapore River Cruises**
Ticket booths at Fullerton, Boat Quay and all the river boat stops (*S$13-18, S$8-10 children; 6336 6111; www.rivercruise.com.sg*).

**HiPPO River Cruise**
Ticket booths at Clarke Quay and Esplanade (***S$15, S$9 children; 6338 6877; www.ducktours.com.sg***).

### Bus Tours

**HiPPOtours**' hop-on, hop-off buses operate from 9am–10pm (individual route times vary), with buses running every 25mins from 34 stops in the city, on five unique 1hr tours. Each tour has live commentary on board. The **Singapore Sightseeing Pass** gets you on all of the routes, with a per day charge (***S$33, S$17 children; 6338 6877; www.ducktours.com.sg***).

### Wartime Singapore

Singapore's historical sights include more than just WWII museums. **Fort Canning★★** and the **Battle Box★★** (*see COLONIAL DISTRICT*) provide an excellent introduction to the era.

Sentosa island (*see FAMILY FUN*) is home to Singapore's largest and best-preserved military installation, **Siloso Point★★** (site of one of the greatest British military follies in Singapore). At **Fort Siloso★★** *(33 Allanbrooke Road; open daily 10am–*

*6pm; S$8, S$5 children; 6275 0388; www.sentosa.com.sg)*, the sole remaining British coastal battery in Singapore, take a free guided tour ***(weekends 11am & 4pm).*** Here, artillery guns, film clips documents and photographs bring history alive; be sure to leave time to explore the **tunnels★**.

In Western Singapore, two sites give an evocative snapshot of former battlegrounds of the western front of the Japanese invasion, as it encircled the British retreat to the south. Northwest of Sentosa, and west of HarbourFront, Labrador Park is the site of the **Labrador Secret Tunnels★** *(Labrador Villa Road; open daily 9am–7pm; S$8 S$5 children; 6339 6833)*. In Pasir Panjang, **Reflections at Bukit Chandu★★** *(31K Pepys Road; open Tue–Sun 9am–5pm; S$2; 6375 2510; www.1942.org.sg)* is a repository of WWII memorabilia, from the British surrender to life in the POW camps. The Japanese set up their headquarters at the Art Deco-style **Old Ford Factory★** in northern Singapore, while their infamous prison was sited in the east at **Changi★**. For a guided tour of Singapore that focuses on this period of history, try the **Changi Museum War Trails** *(S$38; 6214 2451; www.changimuseum.com)*.

## SINGAPORE'S NATURE RESERVES

One of the best reasons for jumping into a hire car and escaping the city centre is Singapore's nature reserves (as well as **Singapore Zoo★★★** and **Night Safari★★★**). The home of so much glass and concrete, Singapore has a higher number of different species of tree than the whole of North America. The inner parts of the island remain as natural rain forest and conservation efforts are ensuring future generations will enjoy the green spaces in years to come.

In Northern Singapore, the main nature reserves are the **Central Catchment Nature Reserve★★** (including **MacRitchie Reservoir★**), **Bukit Timah Nature Reserve★★** *(see PARKS, GARDENS AND RESERVES)* and **Sungei Buloh Wetland Reserve★★**. In Western Singapore is Labrador Nature Reserve, and in the east lies another wilderness, Pulau Ubin.

### MacRitchie Reservoir★

The highest profile developments are at **MacRitchie Reservoir**, where an HSBC-sponsored treetop suspension walkway has been created for observing the high levels, or the canopy, of the rain forest. From the park entrance, the full trail is 11km/7mi long; the walkway is some 25m/82ft above the forest floor at its highest point. To date research *(on Mondays when*

©Singapore Tourism Board

*Bukit Timah Nature Reserve*

*the walkway is closed)* has led to the discovery of 80 varieties of birds, including the Drongo Cuckoo, the Thick-Billed Green Pigeon and Green Leafbirds. From the reptile kingdom comes the Black-Bearded Dragon and the Clouded Monitor. It's a fascinating insight into an otherwise inaccessible world *(see PARKS, GARDENS AND RESERVES)*.

### Pulau Ubin Island★

Worthy of a day trip is the island to the northeast of Singapore, **Pulau Ubin**. Like the treetop walk and the green corridors *(see below)*, the island is being carefully managed to provide natural history enthusiasts with a look into the sea world that exists on the island. The traditional ***kampong*** stilted house standing in the water is still used for families of the fishermen; the old ways are being preserved. Walking trails, cycling trails with bicycle rental, camp sites and chalets are being introduced so as not to spoil the natural beauty of the island. The real gem of Pulau Ubin is the beach area on the northern side, at **Chek Jawa**. It's possible to visit Chek Jawa only at low tide; the number of visitors is restricted to a first-come-first-served basis. The marine life seen here includes horseshoe crabs, starfish, sea anemones and colourful sponges. For more information, access www.nparks.gov.sg.

*Children kayaking on Pulau Ubin*

©Singapore Tourism Board

### Bukit Timah Nature Reserve★★

A visit to the **Bukit Timah Nature Reserve** in the centre of Singapore is a must for anyone interested in seeing tropical rain forest coexist with a modern city. The reserve is the largest natural feature of the island *(see PARKS, GARDENS AND RESERVES)*.

### Sungei Buloh Wetland★★

The mangrove swamps of **Sungei Buloh** are an important site for the observation of migratory birds. Kingfishers and heron also abound here. The reserve has been developed for visitors, and it is possible to walk through the mangrove swamps by way of wooden walkways.

### Green Corridors

A government initiative, the **Park Connector Network** is creating corridors of greenery that link all of the parks, gardens and green areas of Singapore in order to improve opportunities for walkers and cyclists. The routes will eventually cover 300km/186mi of the island, although visitors will probably not reap the benefit of the green shortcuts between housing estates, MRT stations and shops. For more information, access www.nparks.gov.sg.

There are some excellent opportunities to see wildlife in Singapore, both in a "captive" situation and out in their natural habitats. To see Singapore's dwindled indigenous species, it's best to visit the reserves, and in particular the walkway in MacRitchie Reservoir. **Singapore Zoo★★★** and **Jurong Bird Park★★** give a multi-million dollar interactive snapshot of the world's wildlife.

## ISLAND HOPPING
### Two Days on the Southern Islands★

Singapore's main attraction lies in its cultural centre and nature reserves. Its beaches, meanwhile, suffer somewhat from the impact of traffic on the Straits shipping routes. The southern islands south of the island resort of **Sentosa★** provide a welcome break from the city and tend to enjoy better weather.

On the first day, cross over to Sentosa from HarbourFront and enjoy the many attractions there. Stay overnight on Sentosa *(see HOTELS)* and head to **Kusu** or **St. John's** island the next day.

**Singapore Island Cruise** *(S$15, S$12 children; 6534 9339; www.islandcruise.com.sg)* provides ferry service to Kusu and St. John's from Marina South Pier. **Vessel charter** to Lazarus, Pulau Hantu and Sisters' islands is available from Marina South Pier at the ferry departure point.

Be sure that you have a departures timetable for your return journey to Marina South Pier. Keep an eye on the time or you just may have to spend a night under the stars.

## Quick Trips

**Stuck for ideas? Try these:**

# CALENDAR OF EVENTS

Listed below is a selection of Singapore's most popular annual events (dates and times vary; check in advance). For more details call, or access online, the Singapore Tourism Board: (65) 6736 6622 or www.visitsingapore.com. Sports fans will want to check out the **Formula 1™ Grand Prix** in September (*see OUTDOOR ACTIVITIES*).

## JANUARY/FEBRUARY

### Pongal Harvest Festival

A Hindu celebration held at the Sri Srinivasa Perumal Temple in Little India. Starts at 6.30am and lasts four days, with offerings of vegetables, rice and spices to the gods (*6298 5771*).

### Chinese New Year

A two-day holiday with parades, special events and family reunions. Festivities are held before the actual days of the New Year. Gifts of mandarin oranges are taken to family members and ***hang baos*** (red packets of money) to the children. Food stalls in Chinatown sell barbecued pork and ***yu sheng***, a salad symbolising prosperity for the coming year (*6736 2000*).

*January: Sichuan opera during Chinese New Year*



### Thaipusam

This procession from Sri Srinivasa Perumal Temple in Serangoon Road serves as a mark of thanksgiving for Hindu devotees. Entranced participants attach various objects to their bodies with skewers, spikes and hooks (the event is not for the faint-hearted). The procession ends at the Sri Thandayuthapani Temple on Tank Road (*6298 5771*).

## MARCH

### Birthday of Lao Zi

The birthday of Lao Zi, founder of Taoism, is celebrated in Taoist temples of the city. This event involves elaborate Taoist rituals combined with exhibitions of Taoist art and artefacts (*6295 6112; www.taoism.org.sg*).

### Singapore Fashion Festival

Held over a two-week period, this show features top designers and fashions from Europe. During this fortnight, the larger stores offer special promotions aimed at fashion-conscious locals and visitors (*6736 2000; www.singaporefashionfestival.com.sg*).

## APRIL

### Qing Ming Festival

Many Chinese visit temples on this day to clean the tombs of their deceased ancestors. The Chinese temples are busy with people armed with brooms to sweep the graves clean and pay their respects to their ancestors. The best place to see the ceremonies is Kong Meng Temple, Sin Ming Avenue, Chinatown.

### Good Friday and Easter

Celebrated by the Christian community in Singapore at the various churches across the city. At St. Joseph's Church in Victoria Street, there is a Catholic procession on Good Friday.

### Singapore Sevens Rugby

One of the World Rugby Sevens Series featuring teams from New Zealand, Australia, Fiji, South Africa and England (*6469 5955; www.singaporesevens.com*).

### Singapore International Film Festival

This festival, one of the more established celebrations of cinema in Asia, showcases regional and international films at a variety of venues, including The National Museum and Singapore Polytechnic (*6348 5555; www.sistic.com.sg; www.filmfest.org.sg*).

### Singapore Airlines International Cup

Hosted at the Singapore Turf Club, this thoroughbred horse race is regarded as one of the top Asian races (*Singapore Turf Club; 6879 1000; www.turfclub.com.sg*).

### International Polo Tournament

Renowned international polo players take part in this high-profile event at the Singapore Polo Club, one of the oldest clubs in Singapore (*80 Mount Pleasant Road; 6854 3976; www.singaporepoloclub.org*).

### World Gourmet Summit

A gourmand's feast served by international superstar chefs and local leading lights (*6270 1254; www.worldgourmetsummit.com*).

## MAY

### Vesak Day

This important day in the Buddhist calendar celebrates the Buddha's enlightenment and entrance to Nirvana. Devotees release captive birds as a sign of respect for all living creatures. Good places to see the festival are the Buddhist Lodge on River Valley Road, Lian Shan Shuang Lin Temple at Jalan Toa Payoh (*6376 2000*), and the Buddha Tooth Relic Temple in Chinatown.

### Singapore Arts Festival

This arts festival, held usually from the end of May to July, concentrates mainly on Southeast Asian music, dance and theatre, with performances by regional and international participants (*6837 4622; www.singaporeartsfest.com*).

### Great Singapore Sale

*(May to July). See SHOPPING.*

## JUNE

### The Lion City Marathon

This event is open to a wide range of athletes. The full marathon is just over 42km/26mi and starts in waves from 4am through to 6am (*www.lioncitymarathon.com*).

### Dragon Boat Festival

This colourful competition among teams of dragon boat rowers on the river is based on the legend of Qu Yuan (*6736 6622; www.visitsingapore.com*). *See SPECTATOR SPORTS.*

## JULY

### Singapore Food Festival

The Singapore Tourism Board organises gourmet workshops, themed dining experiences and food trails that last an entire month. Regional and international food is on offer (*6273 2998; www.singaporefoodfestival.com*).

### Heritage Festival

Food, music and entertainment are showcased as a way to demonstrate the diversity of Singapore's cultures (*www.heritagefest.org.sg; 6736 2000*).

## AUGUST/SEPTEMBER

### Festival of the Hungry Ghost

The Chinese believe hungry ghosts return to earth in the 7th lunar month. Food, candles and incense sticks are offered to appease them; Chinese operas or *wayangs* are performed to entertain them (*Chinatown; 6736 2000)*.

### The Mooncake Festival

With feasts, lantern displays and pastries called mooncakes, this festival commemorates the 14C uprising against the Mongols during China's Yuan dynasty, when rebels hid their plans for revolt on pieces of paper in mooncakes. The event takes place around Sago Street, where stalls sell Chinese tea and mooncakes filled with lotus paste and melon seeds (*Festival Street market, Chinatown; 6736 2000*).

### Singapore Open Golf Championship

Asia's richest tournament attracts top international players to the Serapong Par 71 course at Sentosa Golf Club (*Sentosa Golf Club; 6275 0090; www.sentosagolf.com*).

### Hari Raya Puasa

After the month of fasting during Ramadan, Muslims celebrate in the Geylang district. Roadside stalls sell snacks, accessories and costumes, and on the main day, men attend special prayers at the mosque (*Geylang Serai; 6736 2000*).

### Formula 1™ Grand Prix

*(6738 6738; www.singaporegp.sg)*. *See OUTDOOR ACTIVITIES.*

## OCTOBER/NOVEMBER

### Birthday of the Monkey God

Not for the faint-hearted, this event features a procession along Seng Poh Road in which entranced mediums slash themselves with blades. Celebrations include the rocking of a sedan chair held aloft by devotees. The chair rocks as if possessed by the Monkey god (*Qi Tian Gong Temple; 6736 2000*).

### Navarathri Festival

Dance and Indian music are performed at the various Hindu temples of the city. The three

**Chingay Parade of Dreams**

The Chingay Festival is a huge parade held at Marine Parade around the time of Chinese New Year. The floats and participants come from all over Southeast Asia. There are free areas to watch the procession, and also grandstand seats. The cost varies from S$30 upwards depending on the position of the stands.

Hindu goddesses Durga, Lakshmi and Saraswati are honoured at this festival, which lasts over nine nights, with three segments for each god. On the 10th night there is a procession led by a grey horse (*Little India Temples; 6736 2000*).

### Theemithi Festival

At the traditional firewalking ceremony in honour of the goddess Draupadi, barefoot Hindu devotees traverse 4m/13ft of hot coals. The festival starts late in the evening at Sri Srinivasa Perumal Temple; to watch the firewalking, be at the Sri Mariamman Temple by 3am (*6736 2000*).

### Deepavali (Diwali)

The Festival of 1 000 Lights is one of the most important in the Hindu calendar. Homes are lit with oil lamps in celebration of Lord Krishna's victory over Narakasura. Shops and stalls in Little India buzz with the sale of saris, perfumes, spices and jewellery (*Little India; 6736 2000*).

### Buskers' Festival

This gathering of jugglers, comedians, musicians and acrobats takes place along the riverbanks in an annual extravaganza of impromptu performances. Apart from traditional busker music, there are stunt artists ready to entertain in this action-packed event. Venues include Clarke Quay, Robertson Quay, Marina Square and Orchard Road (*6736 2000*).

### Hari Raya Haji

This day, one of the most important in the Muslim calendar, commemorates the pilgrimage to Mecca. In Singapore after the morning prayers, sheep and goats are slaughtered as sacrifices, and the meat is distributed to worshippers and the poor (*6736 2000*).

### Singapore Sun Festival

Join artists, chefs and musicians at this arts and lifestyle festival held by the river and at Marina Bay (*www.singaporesunfestival.com; 6536 0031*).

## DECEMBER

### Christmas in the Tropics

Christmas in Singapore is a time to put out decorations and have a good time. The Christmas Light-Up at Orchard Road and Marina Bay is the longest Light-Up in the region, with decorated shop windows, mall decorations, extended shopping, concerts, Christmas trees, countdown parties and more. Churches hold services; Catholic churches hold Midnight Mass (*www.visitsingapore.com; 6736 2000*).

*Dancer in Deepavali*

# PRACTICAL INFORMATION

## WHEN TO GO

Singapore lies 137km/85mi north of the **equator**. Its steady temperature range, between 23°C/73°F and 30°C/86°F, makes it a year-round tourist destination. The atmosphere can be very humid, and in November and December **monsoon rains** are likely. The humidity is such in Singapore that heavy rainfall is a risk year-round; downpours can be short, however. The typical monthly rainfall in Singapore ranges from 170mm/6.7in in July to 260mm/10.2in in January. In between the monsoons, there are frequent afternoon thunderstorms; the average probability of one is about 40 percent on any day, rising to 67 percent in April. Although the **humidity** is high all year, averaging 84 percent, temperatures are generally more stable and lower than one might expect, ranging mostly between 23°C and 30°C (73°F and 86°F). If you plan your visit to coincide with one of Singapore's **festivals**, bear in mind that lodgings need to be booked far in advance, especially during the Chinese New Year, Hari Raya Haji, and Christmas celebrations as well as major sporting events like the **Formula 1 Grand Prix.** If you love to shop, visit in May–July for the **Great Singapore Sale** *(see SHOPPING)*.

Since Singapore has such a warm and humid climate, the best clothes to wear are light cottons. An umbrella is always useful; it can double as a parasol, a popular accessory among Singaporeans. Bottled **drinking water** is a must here, since the heat and humidity can quickly lead to dehydration. Visitors unaccustomed to these humid conditions may find themselves quickly tired. Plan to take plenty of breaks during the day.

## KNOW BEFORE YOU GO

### Useful Websites

**www.visitsingapore.com** – The Singapore Tourism Board's informative, comprehensive site.

**www.nparks.gov.sg** – Singapore's nature reserves are run by the National Parks Board. The website includes maps and visitor information.

**www.timeoutsingapore.com** – The Singapore edition of this online magazine features events, entertainment, restaurants, gigs and clubs.

**www.dpa.org.sg** – This site gives accessibility details for the less able visitor to Singapore.

**www.smrt.com.sg** – The Mass Rapid Transit authority site has information on the excellent integrated transport system on the island.

**Average Seasonal Temperatures in Singapore**

| | Jan | Apr | Jul | Oct |
|---|---|---|---|---|
| Avg. High | 29°C/85°F | 32°C/89°F | 31°C/87°F | 31°C/87°F |
| Avg. Low | 23°C/73°F | 24°C/75°F | 24°C/75°F | 24°C/75°F |

## Tourism Offices

**www.visitsingapore.com** – It's well worth contacting the Singapore Tourism Board in your own country prior to arriving. STB has offices worldwide.

**In India** – Singapore Tourism Board, Ispahani Centre, 123/124 Nungambakkam High Road, Chennai, 600 034, India +91 (44) 4213 9995.

**STB Visitor Centres in Singapore** – Singapore Changi Airport; Arrival Halls, Terminal 1, 2 and 3; 6am–2am daily.
Singapore Orchard Road, Junction Cairnhill and Orchard Roads, 9:30am–10:30pm daily, Nearest MRT Station: Somerset (NS23).

**STB Touristline** – Operating Hours: 8am–9pm daily, 1-800-736-2000 (toll-free in Singapore only), (65) 6736 2000 (Overseas).

## International Visitors

### Singapore's Embassies Overseas

Singapore has High Commissions in India and most other Asian countries, as well as in the UK, the USA, Australia, South Africa, and Europe (*www.embassiesabroad.com*).

**Singapore Consolates in India**

**Mumbai** – 101, 10th floor Maker Chambers IV 222, Jamnala Bajaj Road, Nariman Point, +91 (22) 2204 3205, www.mfa.gov.sg/mumbai

**New Delhi** – N-88, Panchsheel Park, +91-(11) 5101 9801 or 5101 9804, www.mfa.gov.sg/newdelhi

**Chennai** – 17-A North Boag Road, T. Nagar, 600017, Tamil Nadu, +91 (44) 2815 8207 or 2815 8208, www.mfa.gov.sg/chennai

### Foreign Embassies in Singapore

**American Embassy** – 27 Napier Road, Singapore 258508, 6476 9100, www.singapore.us embassy.gov

**British Embassy** – 100 Tanglin Road, Singapore 247919, 6424 4250, www.britain.org.sg

**India Consulate** – High Commission of India, 31 Grange Road, Singapore 239702, 6737 6777, www.embassyofindia.com

### Entry Requirements

A valid passport with at least **six months' validity** is required for entry to the Republic of Singapore; tourists will be granted a social visit pass for 30 days.
There are visa requirements for a number of nationalities such as India, Pakistan and most Middle Eastern countries. Check with the Singaporean consulate in your country for requirements.
Immigration may ask to see a ticket showing departure from Singapore, and they may also ask to see the boarding ticket stub from the incoming flight.
For a full explanation of the entry and visa requirements for Singapore go to: www.mfa.gov.sg.

### Singapore Customs

Goods **prohibited** from being brought into Singapore are: chewing gum (except dental and medicated gum), chewing tobacco and imitation tobacco products, cigarette lighters of pistol or revolver shape, firecrackers, controlled drugs, obscene articles and publications, and reproductions of copyrighted media. For details and a full listing of prohibited items, access *www.*

*customs.gov.sg.* Liquor and alcohol are among items brought into Singapore for which **duties** must be paid; and certain items such as video games, weapons, medicines, and meat products may not be brought in without a permit. *Before you depart for Singapore, be sure to see the full listings of prohibited, dutiable and controlled items online at www.customs.gov.sg.*

### Tourist Refund Scheme

Visitors may be entitled to a refund of the Goods and Services Tax (GST) on goods purchased in Singapore from participating retailers and goods brought out via Changi or Seletar airports. Check online to see if your purchases are eligible: *www.customs.gov.sg.* For fast processing of claims, go to the Singapore location on *www.premiertaxfree.com*.

### Health

**Before You Go** – The advice from the health authorities is that visitors should have the recommended inoculations before arriving in Singapore. There has been concern about the various virus problems of Southeast Asia, such as bird flu and SARS. These problems are just about under control in the region.

**Bites and Stings** – The dengue mosquito is still a current health issue. The Singapore government agency (NEA) has a programme in place to advise the population of Singapore on preventative measures, such as making sure stagnant water is thrown away, and not offering opportunities for the mosquito to breed. It is strongly advised to use mosquito repellent before visiting nature reserves. For information on the mosquito-transmitted dengue fever, go online to www.dengue.gov.sg, but do not be put off visiting Singapore!

**Sanitation** – Bottled drinking water is a must when exploring Singapore, since the heat and humidity can quickly lead to dehydration.

**Health Services** – Many hotels have a doctor on-call 24hrs. **Doctors** are listed in the Yellow Pages of the Singapore telephone directory.

**Ambulance**: Dial 995 for an ambulance.

There are several international health services available to tourists.

**Singapore Health Services** (SingHealth) International Medical Service, Singapore General Hospital, Block 6 Level 1, Outram Road, Singapore 169608; 6326 5656; www.sgh.com.sg.

Pharmacies may be found in supermarkets, department stores, hotels and shopping centres. Registered pharmacists generally work from 9am to 6pm.

### Immunisation

The recommended inoculations for Singapore are: Yellow Fever, Hepatitis A and B, Diphtheria, Rabies, Tetanus, Typhoid.

## GETTING THERE AND GETTING AROUND

### By Air

**Changi Airport** – *6542 1122 or 6344 2733. www.changiairport.com.* The primary international airport for Singapore is Changi, on the eastern coast of the island, about a 30-minute drive from the city centre. Regarded by many travellers as the best airport hub

in Asia, Singapore Changi has retained its enviable reputation as number one in the region with some 80 major and regional airlines flying in and out of here. Singapore Airlines' fleet has the largest number of routes.
Changi has three main terminals and a budget terminal. Terminals 1, 2 and 3 are used by the major airlines, with Singapore Airlines operating from Terminals 2 and 3. After immigration and customs, there are exchange counters, hotel information desks and reservations, as well as taxis, shuttles, buses and the MRT (*see By MRT*) to the city.
Transit passengers who have at least 6 hours to spare can take the free City Shuttle to town.
**Airport Tax** – A passenger service charge of S$21 should be incorporated in the airline ticket (including tickets issued outside Singapore). If not, you may be required to pay the charge during check-in.
**Airlines** – A number of airlines service Singapore Changi from major cities in India. Listed below are several:

- **Air India**
  5 Shenton Way, #B1, 10-12
  UIC Building
  Singapore 068808
  6225 9411
  www.airindia.com
- **Singapore Airlines**
  #02–38/39 The Paragon
  290 Orchard Road
  Singapore 238859
  6223 8888
  www.singaporeair.com
- **Thai International Airways**
  #02–00 The Globe
  100 Cecil Street
  Singapore

*Changi Airport, Terminal 4*
©Singapore Tourism Board

  6210 5000
  www.thaiair.com
- **Jet Airways**
  via Tourmasters Ltd.
  #13-01 112 Robinson Road
  Singapore 068902
  6227 0222
  www.jetways.com/sg

Budget airlines operate out of Terminal 4 at Singapore's Changi Airport:
**Tiger Airways** – Budget flights from Bangalore and Chennai, India, to Singapore. www.tigerairways.com.

**Tipping at Airport** – Tipping is prohibited at the airport. Tipping is not a way of life in Singapore.

### Airport Transfers

**Taxi** – Metered taxis wait outside the terminals; the peak period is 6pm–8pm. Shared minivan taxis are available from booths inside the airport, with fares of about S$8 per person (a regular taxi from Changi to the city centre costs S$18–38 and takes about 30min);

**Crossing the Line**

Jaywalking is illegal in Singapore, so always cross the street at marked crossings. Crossings often have digital countdown timers *(see photo on right)* that beep at you as you cross, so you know exactly how much time you have left before the traffic pours through.

J. Gilbert/Michelin

just give the name of your hotel. Be warned, shared taxis only depart once they have enough customers to fill the cabin.

**Shuttle Bus** – There is a hotel shuttle bus service providing direct transport to the various city districts. The districts served are Orchard Road, Marina Square and Chinatown. The bus departs every 15 minutes 6am–midnight to city hotels, and every 30 minutes at other hours. The cost is S$9 one way. For more information, call 6546 1646 (Terminal 1), 6543 1985 (Terminal 2) or 6241 3818 (Terminal 3). The hotel reservations counter can advise which bus drives to which hotel. The difficulty can come when your hotel is last on the route, with stops at six other hotels before you get to yours; this is no fun after a long flight, so it is often preferable to take a taxi. *See By Coach/Bus opposite.*

**MRT** – If you are travelling light, the **Mass Rapid Transit** (MRT) has a link directly to the airport. Bear in mind that your hotel may not be very close to the MRT station, meaning a potential taxi ride from the MRT city centre station. *See By MRT.*

## By Ship

Singapore is one of the world's busiest sea ports.

**Ferries** – There are a number of ferry services operating to and from ports in Indonesia and Malaysia.

- **Penguin Ferry Services**
  #03–43 HarbourFront Centre
  1 Maritime Square
  6271 4866
  www.penguin.com.sg
- **Batam Fast Ferry**
  #03–50 HarbourFront Centre
  1 Maritime Square
  6270 2228
  www.batamfast.com
- **Tanah Merah Ferry Terminal**
  Bintan Resort Ferries
  50 Tanah Merah Ferry Road
  6542 4369
  www.brf.com.sg
- **Changi Ferry Terminal**
  Ferrylink Pte Ltd
  30 Changi Ferry Road
  6545 3600

**Cruise Lines** – Cruise ships arrive and depart from the Singapore Cruise Centre at **Maritime Square**. Cruises, such as a regional six-day trip to the Malaysian island of Langkawi, can be booked here.

- **Star Cruises**
  9 Penang Rd
  #11–08 Park Mall
  Singapore 238459
  6226 1168
  www.starcruises.com

## By Train

The rail services into Singapore leave from Malaysia, with connections directly to and from Kuala Lumpur, the Malaysian capital. The journey time from Kuala Lumpur is six-and-a-half hours at its fastest daytime service, but this is a pleasant way to arrive in Singapore, where the colonial Keppel Road railway station awaits. There are three express services per day to Kuala Lumpur; check the website for more information.

- **Keretapi Tanah Melayu Berhad**
  Malayan Railway Station
  30 Keppel Road
  6222 5165
  www.ktmb.com.my

## By Coach/Bus

Singapore's SMRT bus services are coordinated with the rail system. Buses operate from MRT stations, so there is no need to walk around trying to find the nearest bus stop. There are 74 routes, of which seven offer a night service (NR). Day fares are a maximum of S$2 (night maximum S$4). Ensure that you have the exact fare as no change is given. Pre-charged **EZ-Link** cards (**Singapore Tourist Pass**) can be used on all buses, just tap the card on the reader. SMRT:1 800 225 5663; www.smrt.com.sg

## By Car

Driving in Singapore is relatively stress free, especially outside the Central Business District, where the traffic does build up in rush hours. It is advisable to buy a local map before you travel, or on arrival. Street signs are plentiful and accurate, but the one-way systems and occasionally long distances between junctions can make navigation difficult.

| Car rental companies | |
|---|---|
| Avis | 6737 1668; in Singapore: 800-737-1668 www.avis.com.sg |
| Budget | 6532 4442 www.budget.com.sg |
| Hertz | 6734 4646 www.hertz.com.sg |

### Arriving by Car

Visitors arriving in Singapore by car may be subject to many of the regulations for cars coming from Malaysia. Before renting a car, check with car rental companies as to whether your car woud be permitted to cross from Malaysia into Singapore. The larger international rental companies allow cars to be driven across the border from Singapore to Malaysia, but will not allow them to be taken into Thailand. Taxis or rental chauffeur-driven cars take passengers to the Malaysian border at Johor or farther.

### Rules of the Road

Keep the following in mind:

J. Gilbert/Michelin

*Brown road signs mark attractions*

**For Whom the Road Tolls**

Tolls are payable at booths on the expressways or automatically deducted via a wireless electronic **ERP** (Electronic Road Pricing) charge card box that is fitted to the windscreen of the car. Tolls are payable in the city centre and on major highways from 7.30am to 6.30pm weekdays, and 10.15am to 2pm Saturdays. The charge card, provided by your rental company, also allows automatic payment of parking charges at the car park exit (the norm in the city centre). In residential areas, a national parking coupon scheme allows drivers to buy coupons from mini-markets that are valid in every coupon parking lot and metered bays. Any parking fines have to be paid prior to leaving Singapore.

- International driving licences only.
- Drive on the left.
- Speed limit: 50kph/31mph on all roads and 90kph/56mph on expressways.
- Seat belts are mandatory. Child seats must be used for infants.
- Headlights should be switched on between 7pm and 7am.
- Do not drink and drive.

### Driving in Monsoons

Thick monsoon rains are incredibly hazardous for all vehicles (two-wheel vehicles in particular). In a monsoon rain, stop and if possible park under a bridge or some sort of cover. Wait until the rain stops before continuing your journey.

### Petrol

There are plenty of petrol stations on the main roads and expressways. Foreign debit cards may not be accepted at tills, so carry a credit card or cash.

### In Case of Accident

If you are involved in an accident resulting in personal or property damage, you must notify the local police and remain at the scene until dismissed. Vehicles should be moved if blocking traffic.

**AA 24-Hr Roadside Assistance** 6748 9911.

## By MRT

The **Mass Rapid Transport** (MRT) rail system of Singapore is an efficient and convenient form of public transport. It is easy to use, and offers passengers access to most parts of the island. There are three lines, each colour coded: The **Green** (**EW**) line runs from Changi in the east through the city centre to Jurong in the west. The **Red** (**NS**) line makes a circular route with Woodlands at its most northern point, the nearest station to the Malaysian border. The **Blue Line** (**NE**) runs northeast, and fills the gap between Green and Red to Tampines. For a journey such as City Hall to Jurong, the cost is S$1.60, so it is very cost effective compared to road transport. The vast majority of Singaporeans use the MRT to go to work, and at weekends, take day trips to the more rural parts of the island. Single trip coupons can be bought from a machine, while cheaper fares are available on the stored value cards (**EZ-Link/Singapore**

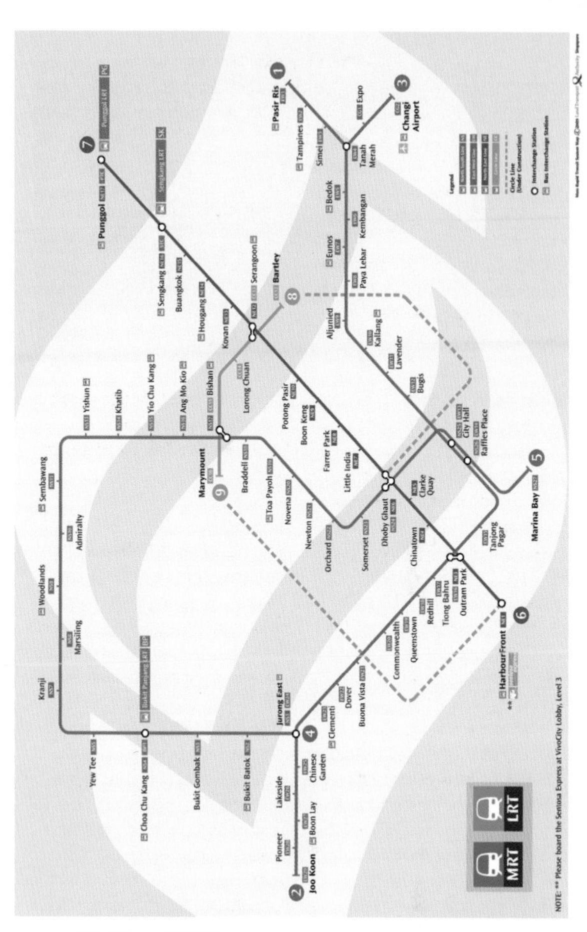


**Ticket to Ride – The MRT**

MRT ticket machines can be used to charge an EZ-Link card *(see By MRT opposite)* and to buy single fares. For a single fare, simply select your language, select "buy standard ticket", then press on the map the station you are going to. The fare pops up, including a S$1 deposit for the plastic ticket, which will be refunded by any ticket machine at the end of your journey (simply insert your card into the machine and collect your dollar). EZ-Link cards can be charged by placing them on ticket machine readers *(shown right)*.

**Three-Wheel Drive**

Originating in Japan, **rickshaws** came to Singapore in 1880, becoming a major form of public transport and a primary source of income for thousands of Chinese immigrants right up to the 1930s. After World War II, bicycle-driven **trishaws** replaced the runner-driven rickshaws. In fact, rickshaws were banned in 1947.

*Travelling by Trishaw*

©Hannes Nimpuno/iStockphoto.com

**Tourist Pass**), which must be purchased from booths (bring your passport). EZ-Link cards cost S$15 (S$10 in value and a S$5 fee). **SMRT:** All MRT Stations: 1 800 225 5663; www.smrt.com.sg.

## By Taxi

Singapore's taxis are generally honest and reliable, and surprisingly cheap. With SMRT taxis you can book online, by phone, or via text message (you need a local SIM card). Booking more than half an hour in advance incurs 70 percent higher fees. Immediate booking is called "current booking". A sign on the windscreen with the name of an area indicates that the driver will only accept customers heading that way. The meter starts at S$2.80; the varied surcharges, including peak rates and ERP charges (*see By Car*), are listed in the passenger cab.

**Comfort/City Cab** 6552 1111 www.cdgtaxi.com.sg
**Premier Taxis** 6363 6888
**SMRT Taxis** 6555 8888; www.smrt.com.sg

## By Trishaw

The trishaw (*see box below*) is a two-seater bicycle-driven rickshaw. Today, the MRT and the affordability of taxis have made trishaws the almost exclusive preserve of Singapore's tourists. Trishaw journeys concentrate around tourist areas and places like Little India and Chinatown's **Trishaw Park** on Sago Street. Tourist prices can be as much as S$10 for a short journey, but you can bargain for a better fare. Group trishaw tours are available.

## By Bicycle

Bicycles can be rented for the city or a ride along East Coast Park, where a flat, straight cycleway borders the sea. Take bottled water to combat Singapore's high humidity levels. In the city centre, you can rent bikes from **Treknology Bikes 3** (*01-02 Tanglin Place, 91 Tanglin Road; 6732 7119; www.treknology3.com*). In East Coast Park, try **Our Family Corner** (*6243 1912*) or **Beach Cabana** (*6344 4773*). Ask at your hotel for further options. Rates generally start at S$4.

# ACCESSIBILITY

For information on wheelchair access and special needs transportation, visit www.dpa.org.sg.

| Important Numbers | |
|---|---|
| Emergency (police, fire, ambulance) | 995 |
| Police | 999 |
| Medical Referral – Raffles International, Patients Centre<br>24hr appointments hotline | 6311 1666 or 6311 1222<br>1222 |
| Dental Emergencies | 995 |
| Pharmacies (emergency) | 995 |
| Time | 1711 |
| Weather | (65) 6542 7788 |

# BASIC INFORMATION

## Accommodations

*For suggested lodgings, see HOTELS.* The Singapore Tourism Board maintains an online **hotel directory**, which indicates which hotels can be booked online, the price ranges and the number of guestrooms.

### Hotel Reservations

Many of the city's hotels can be booked online at Singapore Tourism Board's www.visitsingapore.com.

### Hostels

A great choice for budget travellers. A bed in a dorm-style room starts as low as S$5 in Singapore, which has more than a dozen hostels and low-cost lodgings. For details, www.visitsingapore.com.

## Discounts

Students, children and OAPs often get discounts at attractions; if you are eligible for a discount, you may be asked for personal identification. For a promotional travel and discount pass, visit www.singaporetouristpass.com.

**Jurong BirdPark★★**, **Singapore Zoo★★★** and **Night Safari★★★** also have a combination ticket: contact the local Singapore Visitors Centre: 1 800 736 2000 (toll free in Singapore).

## Laws

The public laws of Singapore are among the most stringent on earth, but the island state is one of the safest tourist destinations in the world. During the incoming flight tourists are prepared for the zero-tolerance policy on drugs by on-board announcements specifying the penalties for importing or trafficking drugs.
**No smoking, eating or drinking** is allowed on the **MRT** or in any public service vehicle. In **public places** such as restaurants, shopping malls, museums, theatres, and cinemas: **No smoking** is permitted.
In general: **No spitting, littering** or **jaywalking**.
**Chewing gum** was banned to keep the streets clean; it should not be brought into the country.

## Business Hours

### Banks

Banks are open Mon–Fri 10am–3pm, Sat 9.30am–1pm and closed Sunday, except for a few in the tourist areas such as Orchard Road. Some banks on Orchard Road are open with the same weekday times on Saturday and Sunday. Most of the island comes to something of a standstill during the Chinese New Year holiday as shops, banks and offices close for the duration.

### Attractions

Attractions such as the nature reserves are open daily usually 9am–7pm, but some open at 6am and close at 10pm or 11pm. Most museums are open daily usually from 9am/10am–5pm or later.

### Shops

Department stores and larger shops, such as those on Orchard Road, are open daily 10am–9pm. The **Mustafa Centre** in Little India is open **24 hours**, as are the convenience stores 7-Eleven. A recent innovation has been that some participating department stores on Orchard Road offer late night shopping Saturday, and these stores are open until 11pm. As a further incentive to customers, the stores offer gifts if a purchase is made between 9pm to 11pm. Check the local press or the STB for further information.

### Pharmacies

Pharmacies are open 9am–6pm. Most of the major hotels have a 24hr on-call doctor service, but in an emergency call 995.

## Electricity

The electricity system is based on the UK, three-pin flat socket, at 220V/60 Hertz supply. Non-UK visitors will need an adapter for two-pin round or flat plugs.

## Internet

The Internet is widely available in hotels, wi-fi hot spots and in a large number of Internet cafes. The island is now the largest free public wi-fi Internet country in the world, with almost all parts of the Central Business District providing access. To find out about free wi-fi in public areas, go to www.visitsingapore.com and click on About Singapore.

## Money/Currency

The **Singapore Dollar** is decimal and comes in notes of S$2, 5, 10, 20, 50 and 100; as well as coins of 1, 5, 10, 20 and 50 Cents, and a 1 Dollar coin.

### Banks

As one of the most important financial centres of Asia, the city has a wide range of banking facilities. The banks on Orchard Road are most familiar with dealing in foreign exchange, and some are open on Saturdays and Sundays to cater to the tourist market.

### Money Changers

Licensed money changers operate all of the exchange counters in the main tourist areas and at Changi Airport.

### Credit Cards

All the major credit cards are accepted in stores, petrol stations and entertainment venues across

MUST KNOW

Singapore, in fact everywhere except in the street markets.
The contact numbers for the credit card companies are as follows:
**American Express** 6880 1111
**Diners Club Card** 6416 0800
**MasterCard** 800 110 0113 (toll free Singapore only)
**VISA** 800 4481250 (toll free locally)

### Traveller's Cheques

Traveller's cheques can be exchanged at all the major banks and foreign exchange outlets. Some banks will not do foreign exchange on a Saturday, but there are plenty of independent exchange facilities around to cash in traveller's cheques.
A commission is charged for the service and your passport must be produced.

### ATM

The ATM network is extensive, given the number of banks around, plus the shopping malls and even the all-night 7-Eleven convenience stores.

### Prices

At one time, the city was famous for inexpensive **electronics**, cameras and other consumer goods. Today, Sim Lim Square still provides decent prices, but know the value of what you are buying in advance (and bargain for it) or you are bound to be ripped off by inflated tag prices. Singapore is also well known for tailor-made linen **suits** at reasonable cost, but seek advice at the tourist office on where to go and what the local prices are before buying a suit.

## Smoking

Smoking is permitted in very few places in Singapore. Stiff fines apply for violation. For a list of prohibited places, check out www.visitsingapore.com.

## Spectator Sports

*See OUTDOOR ACTIVITIES.*

## Taxes and Tips

Singapore levies a 7% **Goods and Sales Tax** (GST) on most goods and services. *For rebate information, see SHOPPING.*
**Tipping** is discouraged in Singapore and is prohibited at the airport. Since most hotels and restaurants add a 10% service charge on customer bills, tipping is not expected.

## Telephone

The public telephone system is provided by SingTel. There are three mobile/cell phone operators active in Singapore: **SingTel**, **M1** and **StarHub**. Local pay-as-you-go SIMs will usually work in your own mobile/cell phone, and will save you money on making roaming calls. Local payphone charges are 10 cents for 3 minutes payable with either a credit card or a stored value card that can be bought at any convenience store, post office or agent. The value cards come in S$2, 5, 10, 20 and 50.

## Water

Singapore's water is very clean, but you may prefer bottled water from convenience stores. Hotels often stock free bottled water for guests (check first with the hotel that it is complimentary).

# THE LION CITY: EAST MEETS WEST

Composed of 64 islands, the Republic of Singapore sits at the tip of the Malay peninsula, about 137km/85mi north of the Equator. Of those islands, Singapore island accounts for 88 percent of the country's size. With a total area of 693sq km/268sq mi, the country is slightly bigger physically than India's Greater Mumbai.

Singapore is the perfect example of **East meets West**—but often not where one would expect. High-flying Chinese sales people strike deals in Paris, yet take *feng shui* advice on how to arrange their furniture for success. A young, urban Singaporean Indian may attend matchmaking sessions in his spare time. Office workers here party just as hard as their counterparts in Spain or New York, but still live with their parents until marriage. This mix of age-old practices with a global mindset typifies how Singaporeans hold onto their traditions in a fast-changing, increasingly international landscape.

For many visitors, the first impression of Singaporeans is that they are obsessed with **money** and **shopping**—preoccupations usually associated with the West. To emphasize that Singapore has more to offer than the opportunity to make money, the island has committed to a relaunch as a "**Renaissance City**", a cultural meeting point between East and West. This government-backed initiative has already borne fruit with projects such as the **Esplanade - Theatres on the Bay**. The fact remains, however, that Singaporeans are more interested in shopping and going out to restaurants than exploring the arts—or until recently, discovering the island's past.

Singapore's **history** has been the main victim of the city's rapid expansion. Only in the mid-1980s did interest in the city-state's earlier centuries soar, but historical mist cloaks its pre-colonial past. Much of the material available

*City in 1940, the National Museum in the foreground*

### The Island's Main Religions

The five main religions on the island, **Buddhism, Christianity, Islam, Taoism** and **Hinduism**, are roughly split along ethnic lines though there is some overlap. Some 51 percent of the population, mostly ethnic Chinese, practice Buddhism, Taoism or some form of ancestor worship. About 85 percent of Christians in Singapore are also ethnic Chinese, with the rest made up of other small ethnic groups. Christianity comes in second at 14.6 percent. Islam is practised by 14 percent of the population, mostly by ethnic Malays and a small but significant number of Indians. Hinduism is practised by 4 percent of the population, mostly ethnic Indians. It is not uncommon in Singapore to see a temple, church and mosque shoulder to shoulder.

until recently has been Chinese reports and European accounts and semi-legendary sources like the **Malay Annals**, commissioned in 1612.

It is estimated that the legendary establishment of the city by **Sri Tri Buana,** the Rajah of Palembang, occurred some time in the 13C. While on a hunting trip, the rajah observed an animal identified by his mentor as a lion (though it was most likely a tiger). The rajah took the encounter as a sign and founded a city by the mouth of the river where he had seen the animal. He called it "Lion City" or **Singapura** from the Sanskrit simha (lion) and pura (city). Ancient Singapura was burned to the ground by the Portuguese during a 1613 raid.

The eventual founding of a British colony in Singapore resulted from attempts to create British bases in the South Seas as far back as the **East India Company** in 1599.

In 1805, 24-year-old **Thomas Stamford Raffles** arrived on the Malay peninsula in Penang (now George Town) to serve the new Governor. He later lobbied for the creation of a British free port on the India–China route, and returned from London with a mandate to found such an outpost. On **29 January 1819**, Raffles arrived in Singapore. The island was populated by Malay fishermen-pirates and a few Chinese. Raffles quickly negotiated a treaty with the local warlord who ruled the island and won concessions for the East India Company. When Raffles finally departed Singapore in 1823, its population had doubled to 10 000, and its trade was higher than that of long-established Penang. Singapore's original prosperity can

### Singapore Fast Facts

**Area**: 693sq km/268sq mi

**Miles of coastline**: 193km/120mi

**City population**: 4.5 million

**Annual visitors**: 10 million

**Year of independence**: 1965

**Form of government**: parliamentary republic

**Airlines servicing Changi:** 80

**Singapore's port:** 600-plus shipping lines

be explained by its status as a free port and its position on the trade route to China. The opening of the **Suez Canal** in 1869 was a further boon to island shipping.

During **World War I**, the British, the Australians and the Japanese worked in concert to dismantle Germany's Far East colonies. The British completed the building of "Fortress Singapore". But the war effort in Europe drained the empire's resources and left Singapore and Malaya underprotected.

At the end of 1941, the defence of Malaya and Singapore was entrusted to **Lt-Gen. Arthur Percival**. The Commonwealth troops consisted of Australian Imperial Forces and 3rd Indian Corps. The RAF had 145 rather old aircraft and the Royal Navy a very modern battleship, a battle cruiser and 4 destroyers. At 12.25am on 8 December 1941, the Japanese 25th Army under **Gen. Tomoyuki Yamashita** landed in northwestern Malaya and two hours later in southern Thailand. The British sent its battleship and battle cruiser north to attack the transport vessels. In one of the most decisive actions of the war, both ships were sunk by Japanese bombers.

From then on, Japanese progress was relentless. By 31 January 1942 the remaining Commonwealth forces had withdrawn to Singapore. Percival, overburdened with Malaya, had not heeded advice to strengthen the island's northern defences. Yamashita landed on Pulau Ubin opposite the shore where Percival had amassed most of his troops. The next day, the main body of the Japanese 25th Army landed on the beaches at **Sarimbun**, while on the 9th, the Imperial Guards landed on **Kranji** beach. For security reasons Allied communications were by telephone only and, as bombardment had broken the telephone lines, confusion reigned. The Japanese proceeded quickly to Bukit Timah, where the biggest battle for Singapore took place; Japanese air superiority was the decisive factor. Low on supplies and water, Percival surrendered on 15 February 1942. Some 130 000 Commonwealth troops were taken prisoner by 30 000 Japanese in the most comprehensive defeat ever for Great Britain. The Japanese occupation was a disaster for the

*East meets West: trishaws with boom boxes and UV lights*

J. Gilbert/Michelin

### What the Future Holds

Betting has always been tightly controlled in Singapore, legal only for horse racing and the lottery. But the government seems to be softening slightly with two brand new "entertainment complexes" in the works, including Singapore's first ever casinos. **Marina Bay Sands**, expected to open in mid 2010, comprises meeting and convention facilities, restaurants, luxury hotel and a casino. **Resorts World at Sentosa**, due for completion in 2010, covers more than 120 acres and boasts Asia's first Universal Studios theme park, the world's largest oceanarium, hotels, and of course, a casino.

British who lost face in Southeast Asia, but it was a greater loss for the Chinese community. Those deemed likely to resist the occupation were driven out into the sea and shot. One of those who escaped was 18-year-old **Lee Kuan Yew**, Singapore's future leader.

In 1945 the British introduced a plan for Malaya's independence. Singapore was to remain a colony, because its naval base was important and because the overwhelmingly Chinese population would make the Chinese the dominant race in Malaya. The real danger that Singapore might become part of the Communist bloc forced the colony to re-evaluate itself. A limited form of self-government was granted in 1955, and the first elections were held in 1959. The winner was the social-democratic **People's Action Party**, led by the 35-year-old, British-educated Lee Kuan Yew, who became Prime Minister.

As Britain started withdrawing from its colonies in the 1960s, a new country called **"Malaysia"** (the 'si' standing for Singapore) would unite the two former colonies, as well as the British territories of Northern Borneo, a combination that ensured the Malays remained in the majority. Singapore was allowed only 15 of 127 seats in the new federal legislature, way below what its population warranted. In 1963 Singapore joined Malaysia, but relations deteriorated quickly.

A divorce with Malaysia was soon formulated, and Singapore became a fully independent parliamentary republic on **9 August 1965**.

PAP has been in power ever since, governing with a strong hand, but also with competence and without the corruption that has mired the region. The city has become a global financial centre. In the first decade of the 21C, Singapore, now governed by Lee Kuan Yew's son **Lee Hsien Loong**, is still a conservative society, with capital punishment, judicial canings, severe drug laws and media censorship.

Despite all that, a solid arts culture has emerged and high-profile projects, such as the **Formula One** night rally in 2008 and the **Youth Olympic Games** in 2010, serve to demonstrate that the ex-colony has indeed entered the New Millennium as the thriving global city it has become.

# DISTRICTS

Singapore's urban area may seem small in terms of physical size (the entire island is 693sq km/268sq mi), but the city concentrates a lot of architectural and cultural diversity into its boundaries. High-rise commercial towers stand next to age-old shophouses, temples and mosques face churches and synagogues, and colonial government buildings flank contemporary condominiums. The major districts of Chinatown, the Central Business District (or CBD), the Colonial District, Little India, Kampong Glam, the Arab Quarter and Orchard Road are themselves divided into separate neighbourhoods or areas, each with its individual character, style and rhythm. The best way to enjoy these districts is to see them on foot.

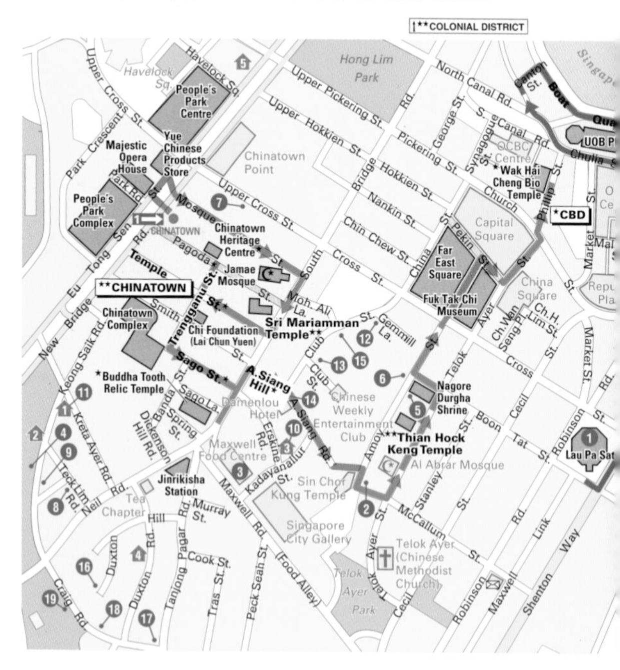


## CHINATOWN★★

Bounded by Boat Quay in the north and the Ayer Rajah Expressway to the south, Chinatown sits opposite the colonial core. On the eastern flank, it's bordered by the East Lagoon Link, Raffles Quay and the Nicoll Highway. In the west it extends as far as Eu Tong Sen Street and the curve of Cross Street that takes in the Subordinate Courts and Ministry of Labour. Chinatown is renowned for its shopping, but recently it has done a lot to make its heritage accessible too.

**Hotels**

1. Hotel 1929
2. Royal Peacock
3. The Scarlet
4. Berjaya Hotel
5. Furama City Centre Singapore

**Restaurants**

**Central Business District**

1. Lau Pa Sat Festival Market

**Chinatown**

2. Amoy Street Hawker Centre
3. Maxwell Food Centre
4. 25 Degree Celsius
5. Beng Hiang
6. Ka Soh
7. Spring Court
8. Tiffin Club
9. Whatever Café
10. Desire
11. Ember
12. Seven on Club
13. Spizza
14. Screening Room
15. Senso Ristorante & Bar

**Tanjong Pagar**

16. Broth
17. Buko Nero
18. Pasta Brava
19. Xi Yan

## Top Three Things to Do in Chinatown

### Go Shopping

Chinatown is a magnet for shoppers. Traditional merchandise to contemporary wares beckon from within brightly coloured shophouses and closely packed street vendors. Based in the old Nam Tin Hotel, constructed in 1900, the **Yue Hwa Chinese Products Store** *(70 Eu Tong Sen Street, open Sun–Fri 11am–9pm, Sat 11am–10pm, 6538 4222, www.yuehwa.com.sg)* calls itself the "one-stop-shop for authentic Chinese goods". As Chinatown's leading department store, It specialises in tea, silk, ***cheongsams***, antiques, and traditional Chinese herbs and medicines across six floors.

*For other stores, see SHOPPING.*

**Touring Tip**

Allow at least three hours for a visit to Chinatown. Better still, start in the morning, have lunch and complete your sightseeing in the afternoon. Don't miss the Sri Mariamman Temple, the food outlets in Smith Street, the shopping in Sago Street and the Buddha Tooth Relic Temple.

**Visit a Place of Worship**
After Singapore became the capital of the British Straits Settlements in 1832, Chinese arrived from mainland China and made their homes along the southern bank of the Singapore River. Though the area was soon nicknamed "Chinatown", it was never an exclusively Chinese area. The mosques and temples here bear witness to Hindu and Muslim immigrants who settled in this busy commercial enclave. They are open to the public, but conservative dress is advised, and head scarves for women visiting mosques are appreciated. *See Houses of Worship (opposite) to plan your visits.*

**Discover Chinatown's Past**
Learn about the experience of early Chinese immigrants at the **Chinatown Heritage Centre★** *(48 Pagoda Street, open daily 9am–8pm, last admission one hour before closure, S$10, 6338 6877, www.chinatownheritagecentre.com.sg).* Occupying three restored shophouses, the centre takes visitors through a different time in the history of Chinatown.
A model junk starts the tour. This flimsy structure is typical of those that brought ***singkehs*** (Hokkien for "China-born immigrant") to Singapore in search of work. A section is devoted to the **death houses** of Sago Street where the sick and old went to die. The tour ends with a re-creation of a crowded Chinatown shophouse, in which landlords were known to cram tenants onto a single floor.
Back on the ground floor, visitors pass a tailor's shop and enter into a traditional ***kopitiam***, where modern-day refreshments can be bought amid period advertisements for Horlicks and Brylcream. Hand-sewn Chinese quilted blankets, clogs and other mementoes can be purchased at the shop. On Telok Ayer Street at the **Fuk Tak Chi Museum** *(see MUSEUMS)*, you can see a model of that street as it appeared in the mid-1800s, when most of the Chinese immigrants arrived.

## Houses of Worship

### Sri Mariamman Temple★★

*244 South Bridge Road.*
*Open daily 7am–noon, 6pm–9pm.*
*Dress conservatively. 6223 4064.*

At the entrance, the technicolour **gopuram** that announces Singapore's oldest Hindu temple features 72 vividly painted gods, goddesses and mythological beasts covering the upper half of the structure (the **sikhara**, or tower). The building beyond the gateway is angled back from the road. Today the temple serves

*Sri Mariamman Temple's sikhara*

J. Gilbert/Michelin

mainly South Indian Tamil Hindu Singaporeans.

The brick substructure of the present building was constructed in 1843 by Indian convicts working under the guidance of craftsmen from Madras. Despite the profusion of decoration celebrating Brahma, Vishnu and Shiva, the temple is actually dedicated to Sri Mariamman, a rural south Indian mother-goddess worshipped for protection against diseases.

In the principal shrine, you will see **offerings** of bananas (a symbol of abundance), mangoes and even saris for the goddess.

The lotus, a symbol of purity and divine birth to the Hindus, is frequently used as a decorative motif.

As you enter the gates of the temple, look up at the strings of fresh mango and coconut leaves hanging above the temple doors—signs of both welcome and purity.

Look out also for the aluminium enclosure into which devotees break coconuts as a symbol of breaking their egos to reveal their pure and kinder inner-selves.

### Thian Hock Keng Temple★★

*158 Telok Ayer Street.*
*Open daily 7.30am–5.30pm.*
*Dress conservatively. 6423 4616.*
*www.thianhockkeng.com.sg.*

*Lighting incense, Thian Hock Keng Temple*

J. Gilbert/Michelin

This Taoist temple, called "Heavenly Happiness", was started in 1821 by Hokkien seamen grateful for safe passage to Singapore. Ironwork was shipped all the way from Scotland, glazed roof tiles from England and the Netherlands, and granite pillars entwined with dragons came from China.

The main hall holds an image of Ma Zhu Po flanked by Guan Gong, the god of war and Pao Sheng Da Di, the protector of life. The **gilded carvings** on the ceiling depict stories from Chinese folklore.

After you pass two traditional Chinese guardian lions and the souvenir shop, there is a **pagoda**, built in 1849 to house Singapore's first Chinese school.

Equally unmissable are the **twin**

**How to Pay Your Respects**

For a visitor there are a number of respectful acts to be completed. As with all Hindu temples, remove your shoes before you enter. At the door ring the bells before entering, thereby asking God to grant your requests. Visitors should also purify themselves by washing their hands and feet, and sprinkling water on their heads. Within the temple compound, walk in a clockwise direction and only encircle the temple hall an odd number of times to bring about good luck.

**dragons** on the temple roof that face each other and represent ying and yang. Look out for the stacks of ancestor tablets in which spirits of ancestors are believed to reside, and in the eastern corner, a small freestanding furnace, always lit, where donations of paper money are burned to placate the gods.

### Buddha Tooth Relic Temple and Museum★

*288 South Bridge Road. Open daily 7am–7pm. 6220 0220. www.btrts.org.sg.*

The modern structure that occupies the block between Sago Lane and Spring Street houses a tooth of the Buddha discovered in Burma in 1980; in 2002 the relic was handed over to be safeguarded in Singapore. Some experts claim, based on photographic evidence, that it is not human at all, but is that of an herbivore. The ground floor is usually open to the public. On level three the **Buddhist Cultural Museum** displays rare artefacts that detail the history of Buddhism. On the same floor, at the rear of the hall, is the **Sacred Buddha Relics Chamber**, where the Sacred Buddha Tooth Relic is housed in a golden stupa of 480kg/1 056lb of 24 carat gold studded with 600 emeralds, rubies and pearls. Tourists and worshippers can attend one-hour daily worship services *(4.30am, 10.30am and 7.30pm)* when the chamber's curtain is raised, but the tooth itself can be seen only on special occasions.

Votive statues, Buddha Tooth Relic Temple

J. Gilbert/Michelin

### Jamae Chulia Mosque★

*218 South Bridge Road. Open daily 5.45am–9.30am. Dress conservatively. A head scarf for women is appreciated. 6221 4165. www.mosque.org.sg.*

Built in 1826 by Chulia immigrants from southern India, this curious building has two tall **minarets**. Two prayer halls occupy a large Neoclassical building set at an angle from the road, like the Sri Mariamman Temple, its neighbour. Though a national monument, the mosque is underrestored, giving a patina of permanence in a city that rebuilds so frequently.
On the tenth day of Dhul-Hijjah, in the last month of the Islamic lunar calendar, Muslims in Chinatown celebrate the annual pilgrimage to Mecca with the sacrifice of goats and sheep in remembrance of the Prophet Abraham. Visitors are welcome to watch; guides on hand explain the ritual.

### Wak Hai Cheng Bio Temple★

*30-B Phillip Street. Open daily 6am–6pm.*

This "Temple of the Calm Sea" was another simple wood-and-thatch shrine where disembarking sailors would express their gratitude for safe arrival.

The temple was built by the Teochew people from eastern Guangdong, who populated this part of Chinatown. Inside, it is divided into two blocks. The one on the left is devoted to Ma Po Cho, the Mother of Heavenly Sages in Taoism, who protects travellers and ensures a safe journey. The one on the right is devoted to Siong Tek Kong, the god of business: both gods remain important in the community. Ceramic figurines and pagodas adorn the roofline, and every nook and cranny of the structure is adorned with tiny three-dimensional reliefs. A **statue** with coins around its neck represents "The Gambler Brother". The Chinese pray to him for wealth and luck, and in the past would put opium on his lips. This custom is still practised today, only now a legal herbal paste called ***koyo*** is used.

## Streets Worth Strolling

### Sago Street★

This street, and Sago Lane nearby, derived their names from the fact

*Joss sticks hanging above a votive kiln*

J. Gilbert/Michelin

**What about Joss Sticks?**

Inside the Wak Hai Cheng Bio Temple, you can buy joss sticks and paper. Three joss sticks are for heaven, your parents and yourself, to be burned before the altar. Three corresponding packets of decorated paper and gold leaf are to be burned outside in the gourd-shaped kilns. The "wishing paper" is four thin sheets stamped with black and red characters. The red sheet is for luck and the others are for washing away your sins, for a long life, and for your wishes to be carried to heaven.

*Temple Street shophouses with Chinese lanterns*

J. Gilbert/Michelin

*Trengganu Street stalls*

J. Gilbert/Michelin

that many sago factories were once located here. By the 1850s the island had nearly 30 factories producing 8 000 tonnes of sago flour a year. By the early 20C, Sago Street had a less salubrious reputation. Along with Smith Street, this was the heart of a red light district until the 1930s. Today, restored shophouses and stalls line the street, engaging in traditional trades like fortune telling, clog making and mat weaving.

*Shophouse near Chinatown MRT*

J. Gilbert/Michelin

**Temple Street★**
In 1908 Almeida Street was renamed Temple Street, partly because of its proximity to the Sri Mariamman Temple and partly because so many streets were named after the d'Almeida family that people died when a fire brigade went to the wrong street. In the 19C, many Malay and Indian homes lined Temple Street, and it was well known for its tinsmith shops. Today quaint two-storey shophouses, renovated as part of the Chinatown conservation programme, flank the street.

**Trengganu Street★**
This street is Chinatown's most bustling thoroughfare, since it connects the area's four main arteries, giving it various Chinese names all meaning "Cross Over Street". In the 19C it was well known for its opium dens, brothels and gambling dens that served the Chinese coolies.
Hawkers were notorious for serving a tonic soup brewed from tortoise, turtle, snake, or lizard. Today, Trengganu Street is part of the Chinatown Conservation Area, with many old shophouses, including some unusual examples with verandas on the upper storey. Look for the **Chinaman Scholar's Gallery** at number 14B, which depicts a home of the 1920s and 1930s.

# CENTRAL BUSINESS DISTRICT★

Singapore's Central Business District (CBD) has come a long way since its 19C beginnings as a swamp below Fort Fullerton, which guarded the river mouth towards Telok Ayer Street in what was then Chinatown's quayside. Today it is the home of Singapore's services industry, a pressurised world of immense skyscrapers that achieves release in the bars and restaurants along Boat Quay. Chinatown and the Financial District overlap with the CBD, occupying the northeast corner of the land south of the river where the Singapore river suddenly curves up towards the Colonial District. Boat Quay acts as a boundary in the north with Merlion Park, Marina South Pier and Clifford Pier marking the district's eastern boundary. To the south and west, the CBD merges into Chinatown proper.

## The Best of the CBD

### Boat Quay★★

In the 19C Boat Quay boomed under Raffles' free-port agreement. By the 1860s three-quarters of all Singapore's shipping business was done at Boat Quay. Shophouses grew along the quayside with the individual height of each building reflecting the owner's personal wealth. Today these structures have been preserved as cafés, restaurants and bars, including the famous **Harry's Bar**. With an eclectic mix of upmarket restaurants, alfresco dining and entertainment spots, Boat Quay is one of the liveliest places in Singapore.

### Fullerton Building★★

*1 Fullerton Square.*

After Fort Fullerton, which stood on this site, was demolished, the 1879 Exchange Building rose in its place. In 1924 a new, larger building housed the Post Office, the exclusive Singapore Club, a reference library and various government offices. During World War II the Fullerton acted as a hospital, and later headquarters of the Japanese Military Administration. After the war the building returned to government use. In 1997 it was purchased and converted into **The Fullerton Hotel**, which opened in 2000 *(see HOTELS)*.

*The Fullerton Hotel*

**Harry's Bar**

*28 Boat Quay. Open Sun–Thu 11.30am–1am, Fri–Sat 11am–2am. 6538 3029. www.harrys.com.sg.*

Just as Raffles Hotel's brand name has been exported round the world, so Singapore has imported Harry's Bar. The original Harry's was set up in Venice in 1931 by bartender Giuseppe Cipriani and his American backer Harry Pickering. As well as being Hemingway's haunt when writing in Venice and the place for the glitterati to be seen, Harry's invented the Bellini cocktail and the seasoned raw meat known as *carpaccio*. This particular tribute to Harry's was founded in 1992 and occupies a renovated waterfront shophouse dating back to the early 1900s. For the last ten years, it has also been a major venue for Singapore's jazz scene. The interior is cooled by ceiling fans and decked out with comfortable rattan furniture.

## The Merlion★

*Located in Merlion Park.*

The bizarre **Merlion statue**, a lion's head mounted on a fish's body, has become one of Singapore's best-known images. Singapura derives its meaning from "lion" (*singa*) and "city" (*pura*) in Sanskrit. The fish tail symbolises Temasek (literally "sea city" in Javanese), the name by which the island of Singapore was once known. Measuring 8.6m/26ft high and weighing 70 tonnes, the cement sculpture spews gallon after gallon of water back into the sea from its mouth.

*Merlion with CBD's skyscrapers*

J. Gilbert/Michelin

## Lau Pa Sat Festival Market

*18 Raffles Quay (Boon Tat Street at Robinson Road). Open daily 24hrs.* *See RESTAURANTS.*

Once the city's only market, this distinctive octagonal-shaped structure was built on land reclaimed from the sea using cast iron shipped in from Glasgow. Today it is a maze of souvenir and food stalls. At night, the side street running alongside it, Boon Tat Street, is closed to traffic and transformed into **"Satay Street"**, with stalls grilling in the open air.

**Fun for Grown-Ups**

On Boat Quay see the fat "Botero Bird", a sculpture by Colombian artist Fernando Botero, have a drink at Harry's Bar and a meal at the ultra-chic Fullerton Hotel, looking out across the river.

# COLONIAL DISTRICT★★

Every visitor gravitates to the Colonial District (or Civic District as it is sometimes known) where the old, genteel buildings of the British combine with the brash modern structures of a confident new nation. During the day, beautiful colonial architecture, green open spaces and lovely views along the Singapore River are juxtaposed with iconic contemporary buildings like the Esplanade - Theatres on the Bay and the New Supreme Court. Evening brings the throbbing nightlife of Clarke Quay and incomparable views of the illuminated skyscrapers of the CBD across the river.

## Explore a Museum

Singapore has a wide range of museums and art galleries. Apart from Western Singapore's **NUS Museums**, which showcase Chinese art, Singapore's main museums—all five of them—reside in the Colonial District. Be sure to visit at least one. Below is a preview. *For a more detailed description of each, see MUSEUMS.*

### Asian Civilisations Museum★★

The museum is of most interest to those keen on Chinese culture and art. Collections include Chinese porcelain and Ming furniture.

### The National Museum★★

This museum prides itself on an innovative approach to presentation. Galleries show Singapore's history alongside exhibits on fashion and photography.

### Peranakan Museum★

This most spectacular of Singapore's museums explores the history and culture of the Straits Chinese, descended from early Chinese migrants.

### Singapore Philatelic Museum★

This museum is a must for postage stamp fans and followers of Harry Potter (there's a collection of Harry Potter stamps from around the world).

### Singapore Art Museum

The Art Museum houses the largest public collection of Southeast Asian art, all in restored school buildings.

**What's What in the Colonial District?**

Bounded by Hill Street, Clarke Quay and Canning Rise immediately north of the Singapore River, the district is the oldest part of Singapore. As late as the 1980s, junk boats and *sampans* were bunched up under the bridges, until a clean-up of the river was undertaken in the 1990s. In the new millennium construction of the New Parliament House, the New Supreme Court, the Esplanade - Theatres on the Bay and the Marina gave the district its current futuristic cityscape. In addition to the Colonial District's many museums, three areas are worth seeing: ◆ Fort Canning ◆ The Padang ◆ Raffles and the Marina. But **a bit of advice**: The Colonial District is the only place downtown where you need bug repellent.

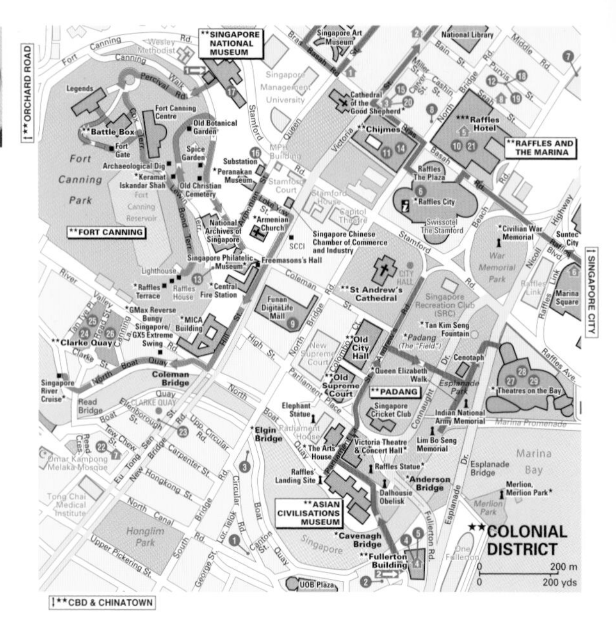


## Hotels

### Centre

1 Carlton Hotel
2 Hotel Grand Pacific
3 Fairmont
4 The Fullerton
5 Raffles Hotel
8 Naumi

### Marina Bay

6 Marina Mandarin

### Clarke Quay

7 Swissotel Merchant Court

## Restaurants

### Boat Quay

1 Molly Malone's
2 Moomba
3 Samarkand

### Fullerton

4 Jade
5 The Lighthouse

### Centre

6 Brotzeit
7 Sofra
8 Asia Grand Restaurant
9 A-roy Thai
10 Empire Café
11 Japanese Dining SUN
12 Yhingthai Palace
13 Flutes at the Fort
14 Lei Garden
15 Szechuan Court
16 True Blue Cuisine
17 Chef Chan's Restaurant
18 Garibaldi
19 Gunther's
20 Inagiku
21 Raffles Grill

### Clarke Quay

22 Ellenborough Market Café
23 Ma Maison
24 Peony Jade
25 Shiraz
26 Coriander Leaf

### Marina Bay

27 Makansutra Gluttons Bay
28 No Signboard Esplanade
29 My Humble House

Fort Gate, Fort Canning

J. Gilbert/Michelin

## Climb Fort Canning★★

The strategic potential of Fort Canning Hill, rising 36m/120ft, was not lost on the British, as it was the highest point close to the river's mouth. It remained the **seat of power** from the time of Raffles, who lived in a bungalow on the hill, to World War II, when Lt-Gen Arthur Percival made it his Malaya Command Headquarters.

### Tour the Battle Box★★

*51 Canning Rise. Visit by 1hr guided tour only daily 10am–6pm, last admission 5pm. S$8. 6333 0510. www.legendsfortcanning.com.*

The star attraction at Fort Canning is the bunker where Lt-Gen Sir Arthur Percival and his staff spent the last days before the Fall of Singapore. Constructed in 1936, his **Underground Far East Command Centre** is a warren of 26 rooms 9m/28ft below ground. During the tour, you will visit 13 of these rooms and through the use of audio, video, realistic sets and slightly dated animatronic wax models, you become a participant in Percival's battle bunker on the day Singapore fell.

## Party at Clarke Quay★★

On Singapore River itself, historic Clarke Quay—where the big marine agencies, ship chandlers' firms and **godowns** (river warehouses) were based—is named after Sir Andrew Clarke, a governor of the Straits Settlements (1873–75). Languishing under disrepair for decades, the quay has been given new life by an extensive redevelopment scheme that has turned it into a prime nightlife hotspot. (There's lots to do in the daytime too.) Best visited at night, the area is a seething mass of people frequenting the back-to-back restaurants, bars and clubs.

## Take a River Cruise★

*The 45min Singapore River Cruise departs from Clarke Quay, Liang Court, daily 9am–10.30pm. S$18, S$10 children. 6336 6111. www.rivercruise.com.sg. Or try a HiPPO River Cruise (www.ducktours.com.sg).* *See IDEAS AND TOURS.*

The first operator to run services on the Singapore river, the Singapore River Cruise company has been running its popular

Singapore River cruise

J. Gilbert/Michelin

**bumboat rides** since 1987. The longer, 45-minute journey is the better value, since it passes below 9 of the 12 river bridges. Speaking of bridges, some of the best **views★★★** of the Civic District and the Central Business District, especially at night, can be obtained from the **Coleman Bridge**, which is the widest of all the Singapore river bridges, and the one that has retained its original 1886 lampposts *(see box page 54)*.

Armenian Church

J. Gilbert/Michelin

## Do a Reverse Bungy

A New Zealand invention that has arrived in Singapore, the **GMAX Reverse Bungy Singapore** is a skywards launch at 200kmh/124mph to a height of 60m/197ft, followed by a scary, yo-yo ascent and fall. The **GX5 Extreme Swing** is less frightening, involving a pendulum free fall of 30m/99ft. Your reactions are recorded on DVD *(for an extra S$15). Clarke Quay, 3E River Valley Road. Open Mon–Thu 1pm–1am, Fri 1pm–2am, Sat 12pm–2am, Sun 12pm–1am. S$60 combo bungy+swing; S$45 single ride. Minimum age 12 years, minimum height 1.2m/4ft. 6338 1146. www.gmax.com.sg.*

## Enter Gadget Heaven

With six storeys full of all kinds of digital communications and computer equipment, **Funan DigitaLife Mall** *(109 North Bridge Road, information counter open daily 10.30am–8.30pm, 6336 8327, www.funan.com.sg)* is Singapore's prime gadget emporium. Prices are very competitive and quality is guaranteed. On the downside, haggling, so common elsewhere,

**What's in a Name?**

Padang means field, and the **Padang★** in this district is proof that money doesn't buy everything. Sitting in the middle of the most desirable real estate in Asia, the sports field lies empty. It is used by the **Singapore Cricket Club** (*see SPECTATOR SPORTS*), which can be seen across the road, and by the **Singapore Recreation Club**, diametrically opposite. Called simply "the Plain" in the 19C, the Padang has traditionally been a ground for parades and political rallies. Before the building of Singapore's National Stadium, it was the focus of celebrations for Singapore's Independence Day.

will most likely get you nowhere. Tourists may want to take advantage of a cash refund counter within the mall that provides an instant tax refund.

## Go to Church

Singapore's oldest church, the small and elegant **Armenian Church of St. Gregory the Illuminator★** *(60 Hill Street, open daily 9.30am–6pm, 6334 0141)* was built in 1835, in the shape of a cross. The original domed roof and bell tower were replaced by a much-criticised Anglican-looking pitched roof and spire in 1853. Oddly enough, the church's interior is round, reflecting the dimensions of the original dome, with a semi-circular chancel and altar. In 1909 it was the first church in Singapore to have electric lights and fans installed.

## Pace The Padang★★

Bounded by Hill Street, Marina Bay and Bras Basah Road, this area of the Colonial District is dominated by major government buildings such as Parliament House and City Hall, the first Christian churches, the Victoria Theatre and other entertainment venues, and sportsfields like the Padang *(see box)*. One of two legendary Singapore hotels, the Hotel d'Europe is no more; it went bust after the 1929 crash and was demolished in the 1930s. In its place stands the Old Supreme Court. The area is a place

*Old Supreme Court*

J. Gilbert/Michelin

of statues, memorials, bridges and hallowed institutions, old and new.

## The Marriage of Old and New

### ◆ Old Supreme Court★★

*St. Andrew's Road. Closed for conversion to a museum.* This courthouse is the last major colonial building (1939) constructed by the British in Singapore. The pediment shows Justice holding balancing scales. Bas-relief panels above the porch depict scenes of the colony's history. There are two domes, but one is not visible from the street. A time capsule to be opened in 3 000AD is buried under the building.

### ◆ New Supreme Court

Sitting adjacent to the old courthouse is this modern courthouse, identifiable by its unusual flying saucer shape.

### ◆ Old City Hall★★

*Closed for conversion to a museum.* Old City Hall (1929) has seen the important events in Singapore's recent history: Admiral Lord Louis Mountbatten's acceptance of the Japanese surrender in 1945, Prime Minister Lee Kuan Yew's proclamation of self-government in 1959, and his declaration of independence from Malaysia in 1965.

### ◆ St. Andrew's Cathedral★★

*11 St. Andrew's Road, open daily 7.30am–8pm, guided tours, 6337 6104, www.livingstreams.org.sg.* This edifice is the third cathedral built on this site (1862). Lightning destroyed the first two. Step inside for a glimpse of the colonial past: ceiling fans, commemorative wall plaques and pews made of teak and rattan.

### ◆ Old Assembly House★

*1 Old Parliament Lane, open Mon–Fri 10am–8pm, Sat 11am–8pm, guided tours, 6332 6919, www.theartshouse.com.sg.* This is the oldest building in Singapore (1827). In 1954 it housed the **Legislative Assembly** of the new Singapore government and after independence in 1965, served as the Parliament House. It is now the **Arts House★**, an arts complex with a cafeteria and a bookshop. The first floor has an exhibit on the legislative history of Singapore.

*St. Andrew's Cathedral*

J. Gilbert/Michelin

*Esplanade - Theatres on the Bay and the river*

J. Gilbert/Michelin

◆ **New Parliament House**
The new House sits behind the Old Assembly House. Outside stands the Elephant Statue *(see box)*.

◆ **Victoria Concert Hall★**
*11 Empress Place, 6338 4401, www.vch.org.sg.* This hall was the home of the Singapore Symphony Orchestra until the opening of the Esplanade - Theatres on the Bay. **Victoria Theatre★★** *(on your left)*, built between 1856–1862, served as the Singapore Town Hall. After the death of Queen Victoria, the second building, the **Victoria Memorial Hall★**, was completed in 1905 in her memory. In 1909 the combined structure opened to the public with a performance of the *Pirates of Penzance*.

◆ **Esplanade - Theatres on the Bay★**
*Esplanade Drive, box office open daily noon–8.30pm, 6348 5555, www.esplanade.com.* Completed in 2002, this complex has been

**Statues of Significance**

The Padang holds three statues worth seeing:

1. **Raffles Statue★**
   - Unveiled on 29 June 1887
   - Moved to this site in 1919
   - Marks the 100th anniversary of the treaty that ceded Singapore to the British
2. **Raffles' Landing Site**
   - The so-called "White Raffles"
   - Erected in 1972 to mark his landing on Singapore island
   - Date inscribed is incorrect (Raffles arrived "on a sandy beach" off Singapore on 28 February 1819, but did not land on Singapore mainland until the next day)
3. **Elephant Statue**
   - An 1871 gift from the King of Siam
   - First placed in front of the Victoria Theatre, but was moved here to make way for the Raffles Statue

**Good Connections**

How many bridges cross the Singapore River? 12 in all.

Though the **Coleman Bridge**, the widest of all the Singapore river bridges, is upstream in the Fort Canning area, the Pandang boasts three bridges of its own:

- The elegant **Anderson Bridge**★ at the entrance to Marina Bay was completed in 1910. It became necessary after the coming of vehicular traffic in the 1900s.
- The later **Esplanade Bridge** next to it (1997) bears witness to the increased traffic growth between the CBD and the Padang districts.
- The **Cavenagh Bridge**★, erected in 1869, is a pedestrian suspension bridge made of steel shipped from Glasgow. It replaced a ferry service that disgusted European residents who had to pay one *duit* (one-quarter of a cent) each way to go to the post office on the opposite bank.

Between the Cavenagh and the Coleman is the **Elgin Bridge**★, where a wooden structure predated even Raffles' arrival. It's the "bridge" referred to by the North and South Bridge Roads that radiate from here.

crucial to a flourishing Singapore Arts Scene. It has a shopping mall, a 2 000-seat theatre, a 1 600-seat concert hall, a smaller recital hall, a studio theatre, rehearsal and practice studios, conference rooms and a performance concourse. With their spiky sunshades, the two domes have been likened to two durians and to flies' eyes. (They are supposed to resemble the texture of rattan and other Asian-sourced patterns.) The popular hawker centre Makansutra Glutton's Bay is right next door.

Raffles Landing Site

J. Gilbert/Michelin

## Raffles and the Marina★★

This is the European area, beyond the Padang's government buildings. It might as well be called the "Raffles district" because of all the places (Raffles Hotel, Stamford Road, Raffles Avenue, Raffles Boulevard, Raffles City) named for Singapore's founder. Land reclamation extended the area to include the giant shopping malls of Suntec City and the Marina, plus the eye-catching Singapore Flyer. The **Formula 1™ SingTel Singapore Grand Prix** course runs around the Marina Bay Area.

### The High Life

Even if you don't want to spend the money to live the high life at the Raffles Hotel, you can get a birds-eye view of it and the city from the can't-miss Ferris wheel.

**Raffles Hotel★★★**
*1 Beach Road. 6337 1886. http://singapore.raffles.com.*
Possibly the most famous hotel in Asia (and one of the most expensive), the Raffles Hotel has captured the imagination of travellers since its creation as a 20-room bungalow in 1887. Celebrated guests include Rudyard Kipling, Somerset Maugham, Noël Coward and James Michener.
In 1915 the hotel became famous for the **Singapore Sling**, a gin and cherry brandy cocktail invented by a barman. It's so popular today that the hotel is the world's largest gin consumer, with 20 000-plus bottles required yearly. The oldest bar, where casually dressed visitors are allowed, is the **Long Bar.**

**Singapore Flyer★★**
*Marina Bay. Open daily 8.30am–10.30pm. S$29.50, S$20.65 children. 6333 3311. www.singaporeflyer.com.sg.*
Modelled on the London Eye, the Singapore Flyer is taller, with a height of 165m/541ft, equivalent to a 45-storey building. It is the world's largest observation wheel. The rotating, air-conditioned passenger capsules, each carrying up to 28 people, offer a stunning view of the Marina, the CBD and on a clear day, the Indonesian islands of Batam and Bintan.

## Malls for the Millennium

**Raffles City Shopping Centre★**
*252 North Bridge Road. Open daily 10am–10pm. 6318 0238. www.rafflescity.com.*
Opposite the Raffles Hotel rise the towers of Raffles City. This 'city within a city' is home to a shopping mall, housing and hotels. The first mall in Singapore built outside Orchard Road, it has become one of the most fashionable shopping and tourist hubs in the city.

**Marina Square**
A shopping mall established around the **Mandarin Oriental** and the **Marina Mandarin**, this is one of the malls that sprang up in Singapore in the new millennium.

**Suntec City**
This mall belongs to a wealthy Hong Kong individual who built it in *feng shui* fashion, with five towers that open like the fingers of the left hand around the **Fountain of Wealth★**. In 1998 the fountain entered the *Guinness Book of Records* as the world's largest. But it won't

*Singapore Flyer and the marina*

Raffles Hotel

Raffles Hotels & Resorts

seem that way if you arrive outside the 10-minute **laser show** *(8pm, 8.30pm, 9pm)* when the water runs down from a huge bronze ring 21m/69ft in diameter supported by four 14m/46ft-high legs. Arrive between 9am and noon, 2.30pm and 6pm, 7pm and 7.45pm or 9.30pm and 10pm for a "touch the water session" when you may touch the water for luck, while circling the fountain clockwise.

## Houses of Many Faiths

The Raffles-Marina section of the Colonial District is home to several places of worship that stand as a testament to the cultural diversity of Singapore. Two have been converted for commercial purposes.

### Chijmes★★

*30 Victoria Street. Open daily 10am–2am. 6337 7810. www.chijmes.com.sg.*

Though today an upmarket restaurant and shopping complex, Chijmes was built as the **Convent of the Holy Infant Jesus** in 1854 by French nuns. The attached Gothic chapel with Art Nouveau stained-glass windows dates from 1903, but it was deconsecrated in 1983 when the convent closed. Check out the convent's corner at Bras Basah Road/Victoria Street from the inside to find the **Gate of Hope** where many babies, especially girls, were abandoned in baskets to be raised by the nuns. Such abandonment was particularly acute in the Year of the Tiger because "Tiger Girls" supposedly brought bad luck to their families.

### St. Joseph's Church★★

*143 Victoria Street. Open daily 7.30am. Weekday mass 6.15pm. 6338 3167.*

This beautiful white-and-cyan church is decorated with exterior tiles depicting stories from the Old Testament and interior wooden panels corresponding to the Stations of the Cross. It marks the site of the Portuguese mission to Singapore, which arrived as early as 1823 *(see box opposite)*. A church was first built in 1853 with a gift from the King of Portugal, but it was torn down in 1912 and the present Gothic-style building was erected in its place. Its most striking features are its octagonal tower and dome.

**Fast Fact**

**St. Joseph's Church** stands on the site of the Portuguese mission to Singapore, which arrived in 1823. The activities of the Portuguese and French proselytising missions were so competitive towards the end of the 19C that they required intervention by the Pope himself, who had to outline their respective spheres of influence.

### Cathedral of the Good Shepherd★

*"A" Queen Street. Open Mon–Sat 7am–6pm, Sun 8am–6pm. 6337 2036.*

Built in 1843–1846, this church is the oldest Roman Catholic church in Singapore. The edifice was designed in a Renaissance Revival style, simpler than St. Andrew's and much less ornate than Catholic cathedrals elsewhere. Its acoustics are excellent, and it contains the oldest operational organ in Singapore, dating from 1912. Sadly organ recitals are few and far between.

### Kwan Im Thong Hood Cho Temple★

*178 Waterloo Street. Open daily 6am–6pm. 6337 3965.*

This Taoist temple draws large crowds; the deity it is devoted to, **Guanyin**, is supposed to answer questions asked of her. The faithful think of the question and shake the joss sticks until one falls down. Each stick has a number corresponding to an answer that can be obtained at the counter. Its congregation also worships next door at the Sri Krishnan Temple.

### Sri Krishnan Temple★

*152 Waterloo Street. Open daily 6.30am–noon, 5.30pm–9pm. 6337 7957.*

The origins of this temple, a popular venue for Hindu weddings, go back to 1870 when a Hindu holy man put a statue of **Krishna** under a banyan tree on this spot in Waterloo Street. A shrine was constructed in 1904, a dome in 1933, and walls in 1959, but the current ornate structure dates from a 1985–89 reconstruction. As a nod to the temple next door, the Sri Krishnan Temple contains an **altar★** to Guanyin, the goddess of Mercy. As a result, many Chinese Taoist devotees visit to worship there. Chinese New Year festivities are held in both temples.

*Chijmes*

### Singapore's Religions

**Buddhism** was evident here long before the other religions appeared. Its influence waned with the spread of Islam before becoming the dominant religion once more with the arrival of immigrants from southern China. **Taoism** and the three major streams of Buddhism are found in Singapore; the Chinese Mahayana form is the most predominant. **Islam** arrived in the 14C and was adopted by the native Orang Laut population. Since then, Islam has been the *de facto* religion of the majority of the ethnic Malay population.

A moderate version of Islam is practised in Singapore: women have to cover only their hair and limbs, which they do by donning the *tudung* (head scarf). **Hinduism** is a relative latecomer to Singapore. It came with the Indian immigrants soon after 1819. It has the smallest number of adherents of the main religious groupings, but some of Singapore's more important festivals are Hindu. After Raffles' arrival, **Christian** missionaries came to Singapore. Their main successes were among the Chinese, evident today by the fact that 85 percent of Christians in Singapore are ethnically Chinese. To serve the small **Jewish** community, there are two synagogues in Singapore, one of which came into being as the result of the settlement of Iraqi Jews in the colony by 1824.

### Bencoolen Mosque

*59 Bencoolen Street. Open Mon–Thu, Sat–Sun 10am–12.30pm, 2.30pm–4pm, Fri 2.30pm–4pm.*

One of the earliest in Singapore, this mosque (1845) at Bencoolen Street is easy to miss since it shares its entrance with a shopping arcade. A victim of the Bencoolen street redevelopment craze, it is being merged with a commercial and residential apartment block.

### Church of St. Peter and St. Paul

*225A Queen Street. Open daily 8.30am (office open Mon–Fri til 7pm). Mass Mon–Sat 5.30pm. 6337 2585. www.sppchurch.org.sg.*

Built in 1870, this church is referred to as the "Mother Church" of the Chinese Catholics in Singapore. It has a congregation that is almost exclusively Asian. As the population shifted out of the city centre, its presence serves to remind us of the mélange of cultures that made up the colony—and still make up Singapore today.

### Maghain Aboth Synagogue

*24/26 Waterloo Street. Open during services Mon–Fri 7.30am, Sat 9am, Sun 8am and by appointment. 6337 2189.*

Meaning "Shield of Our Fathers", the Maghain Aboth is the oldest of the two synagogues in Singapore. It was built in 1878 in the Neoclassical style. The synagogue served a Jewish diaspora that began as a congregation of 40 Baghdad Jews, who had settled in the colony by 1824, and eventually totaled 1 500 by 1939. Enter the inside, where carved teak-and-rattan seats remind visitors of the pews in St. Andrews Cathedral. The balcony for women was added later.

# LITTLE INDIA★★

The regeneration of the city's Indian quarter has brought many new sites to the attention of visitors, as well as a whole new perspective on its culture and society. Majestic mosques are tucked away within narrow streets, while Dravidian *gopurams* struggle to be seen among Buddhist lacquered temple roofs. The streets and the shops are alive with the South Asian bazaar-buzz lacking in the shiny downtown shopping malls. Farrer Park and Rochor Canal border the area, and Serangoon Road is the main thoroughfare. Here are two walking tours that incorporate a selection of attractions in the district.

## Walking Tour

*Follow the blue line on the map to take this 3km/1.8mi round-trip tour of Little India. Allow 60min to 90min. Start at the Little India MRT station.*

### Tekka (Bamboo) Market★

*665 Serangoon Road.*
*Open daily 8am–9pm. May be closed temporarily for renovation.*

The interior of the market and mall is an incongruous sight in a place called Little India, populated as it is with Chinese hawker stalls and fortune tellers next to Indian curry kitchens serving their meals on banana leaves. That chilli crab cooked in Boat Quay was very likely purchased at this big vegetable, meat and seafood market.

**Touring Tip**

Little India and Farrer Park should both be avoided on Sundays when the sheer number of people makes movement difficult.

### Buffalo Road★

As the name implies, buffalo used to be penned here. Today this narrow, fascinating hub of activity offers the quintessential Little India experience. Every other house is a restaurant or spice centre, and every staircase leads to exotic services such as Ayurvedic massage, eyebrow threading or fortune-telling through numerology, nameology or phonology.

J. Gilbert/Michelin

*Gopuram of Sri Veeramakaliamman Temple*

**The Past and Lively Present**

The first group of 120-plus Indian assistants and soldiers who came ashore with Raffles settled among the Chinese in Kampong Chulia. Although Raffles later set aside an area farther up the Singapore river for their use, the community mixed in with the others, as the early Hindu temples in Chinatown readily reveal. Later, the introduction of cattle in the pastures by the Rochor Canal and the construction of brick lime kilns resulted in an influx of more Indians from Calcutta and Madras. Hindu communities mainly settled in the area affectionately called "Little India", while Muslims settled farther up **Serangoon Road**. The unmistakable hustle and bustle of the subcontinent can be felt in the permanently jammed narrow alleys of Little India.

The aroma of open spice sacks mixes with the scent of flower garlands and the smells of a thousand curry dishes. Seamstresses sew clothes placidly in the street, alongside merchants peddling their silks, saris and pashminas as they try to be heard over the soundtrack of Bhangra tapes. Bumping into jewellers and bridal make-up artists, chatting with fortune-tellers and numerologists, sifting through Bollywood DVDs and Hindu fashions: never has strolling seemed more exhilarating. **Don't miss:** the temples, mosque, Buffalo Road or Campbell Lane. Try on a sari, get a henna tattoo or a "Pottu" (a red dot on your forehead, if married).

### Little India's Arts Belt

*Kerbau Road. Open daily 10am–9pm.*

In 2001 Singapore's **National Arts Council** acquired and restored ten shophouses in **Kerbau** ("Buffalo") **Road** and leased them to various ethnic arts and performance groups. As these are teaching- and workshop-based, however, there is little for the visitor to see, apart from a quirky contemporary art gallery at #61, called **Plastique Kinetic Worms★**.

### Chander Road★

Little India's equivalent to Chinatown's Smith Street, this road is lined back-to-back with *Chetinaad* cuisine restaurants offering specialities from south India, such as fish curry.

### Shree Lakshminarayan Temple★

*5 Chander Road. Open daily 6am–noon & 4pm–9:30pm. 6293 0195. www.lakshminarayantemple.com.*

This modern temple, opened in 1969, serves the Hindu community from Uttar Pradesh, Bihar, Punjab and Gujarat. It is built in the simpler, **Nagara** north Indian style and as such, is markedly different from the Dravidian Tamil temples normally seen in Singapore with their extravagantly carved **gopurams**. In this temple it is the **sikhara** (a conical structure above the *sanctum sanctorum*) that forms the architectural focus *(not visible from the street)*. The main festivals celebrated here are the **Birth of Rama**, the **Birth of Krishna** and **Holi**, the **Festival of Colours**.

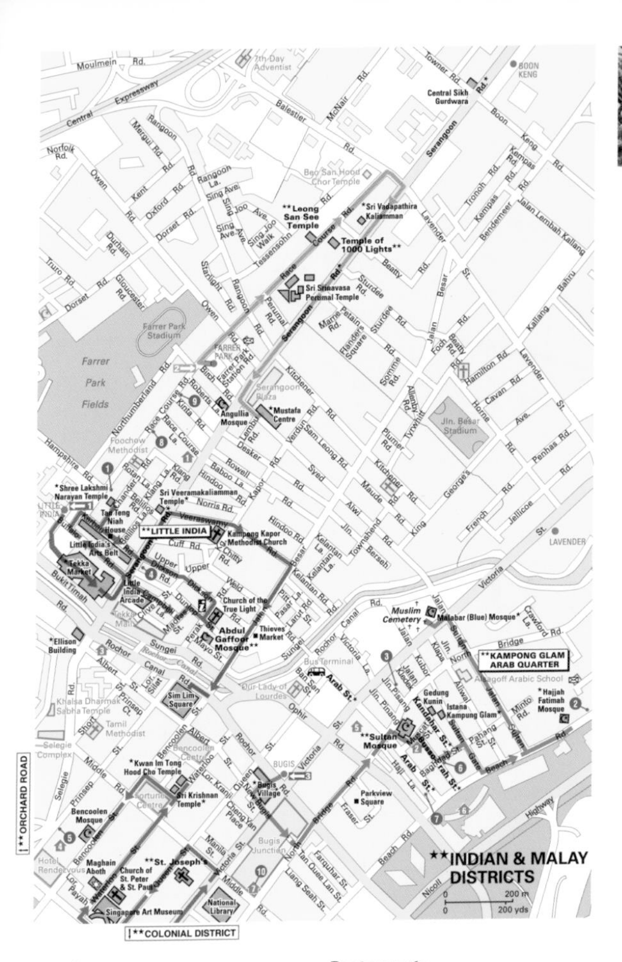


## Hotels

### Little India

1. Broadway Hotel
2. Sleepy Sam's
3. Albert Court
4. Strand

### Kampong Glam

5. Golden Landmark
6. Parkroyal on Beach Road
7. InterContinental Singapore

## Restaurants

1. Banana Leaf Apolo
2. Golden Mile Food Centre
3. HJH Maimaunah
4. Komala Vilas
5. Pho Lan
6. Alatruka
7. Café Le Caire
8. Muthu's Curry
9. Jade of India
10. Man Fu Yuan (InterContinental Hotel)

Abdul Gafoor Mosque

©Lawrence Wee/Dreamstime.com

### House of Tan Teng Niah★

*37 Kerbau Road. Closed to the public.*

One of the few remaining Chinese villas in Little India, this six-room house was built in 1900 for the wife of the owner of a confectionary business and meat-smoking factory. It is painted in the usual vivid colours favoured by the Straits Chinese. Note the second floor **pintu pagar** (ornamental swing doors), the roof overhangs and the calligraphic inscriptions.

### Little India Arcade

*48 Serangoon Road.*
*Open daily 9am–10pm.*

This cluster of shophouses from the 1920s was renovated in the 1980s and holds a variety of Indian shops and eateries. More interesting than the Tekka Centre and Mall, it is a favourite haunt of shoppers looking for bargains. There is a **Cultural Centre** (*closed Sun*) inside offering a short documentary on Little India, a video on Indian culture and an exposition of all things Indian.

### Campbell Lane★★

Named after a member of the managing committee of the Raffles Museum and Library in the 1870s, this lane is another street that offers a full-on encounter with genuine Indian culture. The street originally held slaughterhouses manned by Indian Muslims, as cows are sacred in Hindu culture. Today it is the focal point of the **Pongal** festival and of the **Deepavali** celebrations.

**Little India Festivals**

**Thaipusam**: Celebrated in January/February on the full moon of the Tamil month of Thai. Devotees with shaved heads walk along a set route and sometimes pierce their bodies, tongues or cheeks with spikes to show the triumph of mind over matter.

**Pongal** (Harvest Festival): Around the end of January each year, with festivities lasting four days. On the third day, cows are bathed, their horns polished, and they are made to run through the streets at night.

**Deepavali** (Festival of Lights): Also known as Diwali, this festival celebrates the triumph of Light over Darkness. It occurs one day in October every year, when Little India is abuzz with revellers, lights, music and outdoor bazaars.

**Navarathri** (Nine Nights): This feast in early October is held in memory of the period of nine days and nights when the goddess Durga fought the demon king Mahishasuran. On the tenth day, the statue of Durga is paraded on a silver chariot.

**Roads Well-Travelled**

Three of Singapore's most important roads flank Tekka Market. Separating it from Little India MRT station, **Race Course Road** is a long road that marks the perimeter of the old race course opened in 1843 and operating until 1935 when it was moved to Bukit Timah. On the other side of Tekka Centre lies **Serangoon Road★**, which takes its name from a marsh stork that is called *burong ranggong* in Malay. This is one of the oldest and longest roads in Singapore and was marked clearly on the first city maps as a straight "road through the island". Connecting these two is **Bukit Timah Road,** the preferred abode of expatriate westerners, which starts here and continues well into the interior.

The race course, Singapore's first, was more often than not used by nearby grazing cattle. The course was so central to Singapore's social life that its first century was celebrated there in 1819. It was the site of Singapore's first airfield: in fact, the first plane to fly over Singapore in March 1911 took off from there.

*Sri Srinavasa Perumal Temple*

J. Gilbert/Michelin

DISTRICTS

### Masjid Abdul Gaffoor Mosque★★

*41 Dunlop Street. Open Sat–Thu 9am–1pm & 2.30am–5pm, Fri 3pm–5pm. 6295 4209.*

This elaborately decorated building (1907) is named after a sheik who raised money to replace the dilapidated mosque that had stood here since 1857. Catering to the Indian Muslims who settled in the area, it features Moorish, European and south Indian styles: a stained glass cupola, 22 small minarets, miniature onion domes and Roman and Saracen columns. Don't miss the Arabic calligraphic inscription over the main door in the form of a **sundial**; the names of Islam's chosen prophets are written in its 25 rays.

### Church of the True Light

*25G Perak Road. Open Sat–Sun 9am–1pm (worship service Sat 5pm). 6294 0797. www.truelight.org.sg.*

Typifying Singapore's melange of beliefs, this Anglican church serves the Chinese community in Little India and conducts services in Hokkien and Mandarin. Inside, the Chinese ideogram for "Love" hangs above the altar and verses from the Bible are painted in Chinese over the walls. The exterior bell tower combines Christian and Chinese styles.

### Sri Veeramakaliamman Temple★

*141 Serangoon Road. Open daily 5.30am–12.15pm & 4pm–9pm. 6295 4538. www.sriveeramakaliamman.com.*

Founded in 1835 and originally built in 1855 by labourers who worked in the area's lime kilns, this is one of the earliest Indian temples in Singapore, originally called **Sunnambu Kambam Kovil** (Lime Village Temple). The workers gradually built a shrine which, in the late 19C, was replaced by a wooden temple, followed by a walled structure in the early 20C. The present form of the building dates from 1987. One of the city's many Hindu temples in honour of the goddess **Kali**, this very popular temple venerates her incarnation as Destroyer of Evil. The faithful worship a miraculous statue of Kali that was brought from India in

*Shophouse on Race Course Road*

J. Gilbert/Michelin

1908. Built in the Dravidian style of south India, the gate **gopuram★**, best viewed from across the street, is one of the handsomest and tallest in Singapore.

### Kampong Kapor Methodist Church

*3 Kampong Kapor Road. Open around worship times, Sundays 8am, 9.30am, 11.30am, 2pm, 5.30pm or upon request. 6293 7997. www.kkmc.org.sg.*

Not typically open for tourism during the week, this interesting building was constructed in 1930 in an **Art Deco style** to serve the local Peranakan community. If you find it open, walk in to admire the **stained-glass windows**.

### Veeraswamy Road★

This street runs right through Kampong Kapor, the site of the old lime kilns. It was the home of many Straits Chinese, and has some of the best examples of **Peranakan architecture** outside Katong and Chinatown. Not content with pilasters and elaborate corniches, there are tiled fronts, especially outside numbers 23–27 and 22–36. The two opposing **shophouses★** at the junction with Jalan Besar are particularly interesting as they are set on three floors rather than two, with double balconies and overhanging iron roofs.

### Thieves Market

This market, Singapore's main flea market, clusters around Pitt Street.

### Sim Lim Square

*1 Rochor Road. Open daily 9am–8pm. 6338 3859. www.simlimsquare.com.sg.*

The elder brother of the Funan Centre, this mall is a six-storey IT mall featuring high-tech equipment. The mall operates a free bus service to downtown.

## Farrer Park Area

*Follow the orange line on the map to take this 2km/1.2mi walking tour. Allow 1hr to fully enjoy the sights. Start at the Farrer Park MRT station and take exit B. Walk up Race Course Road. There are some antique shops at #278, #280 and #282. No prices are shown, so why not haggle?*

### Leong San See Temple★★

*371 Race Course Road. Open daily 6am–6pm. 6298 9371.*

This Buddhist temple dates from 1917 when a hut was raised for the worship of a statue of **Guanyin**, the goddess of Mercy. The main temple was completed in 1926 in the Chinese Palace style with

**Touring Tip**

This Muslim Indian complement of Hindu Little India is often overlooked by visitors, but it is full of pleasant surprises. It showcases some of the most beautiful Hindu and Buddhist temples in Singapore and offers round-the-clock shopping in the Mustafa Centre. Serangoon Plaza fills with single Indian men hanging around every Sunday afternoon, and some women may find this slightly intimidating.

Lanterns outside Leong San See Temple

J. Gilbert/Michelin

imported materials; it was built without nails. View it from across the road, so you can see the tiled **roof★★**, which resembles a sea of ceramic dragons dancing around a large blazing pearl. At the back of the building, an ancestral worship hall houses tablets for both deceased monks and laypeople.

### Sakya Muni Buddha Gaya★★ (Temple of 1,000 Lights)

*366 Race Course Road. Open daily 8am–4.45pm. 6294 0714.*

No regular services are held at this Burmese-Thai Buddhist temple, except on **Vesak Day**, but have your fortune told (50 cents) by turning the **Wheel of Life** by the counter. The 13m/50ft high Sitting Buddha is illuminated by 989 light bulbs. Below the statue, the sanctum has a Sleeping Buddha and a statue of the Hindu elephant god **Ganesh**.

### Sri Vadapathira Kaliamman★

*555 Serangoon Road. Open daily 5am–9pm (Fri 9.30pm). 6298 5053.*

Another temple dedicated to Kali, this building was renovated by sculptors and artisans from south India who built its most notable feature, the **double gate**.

### Sri Srinivasa Perumal

*397 Serangoon Road. Open daily 6.30am–12pm & 6pm–9pm. 6298 5771.*

Dedicated to the Lord **Vishnu**, this Indian temple (1855) was built over time; the main structure was finished in the 1960s, the ***gopuram*** in 1979. Walk to the back and admire the pink peacock wedding hall and the canvas-covered **Vasantha Madapam** used to carry the idol of Vishnu in processions.

### Angullia Mosque

*265 Serangoon Road. Open Sat–Thu 9am–4pm, Fri 2pm–4pm. 6295 1478.*

This is one of two mosques built by the Angullia family in the 1850s. Primarily Gujarati Muslims worship here.

### Mustafa Centre★

*145 Syed Alwi Road, off Serangoon Road. Open daily 24hr. 6295 5855. www.mustafa.com.sg.*

A Singapore institution, this department store caters to the budget shopper without sacrificing quality.
Continually expanding, it is now spread over six levels and 6 500sq m/70 000sq ft. There's a money-changing service open even at 2am on Sunday morning.
For serious shoppers, a "Shop and Stay" service is available in a 130-room hotel.

## KAMPONG GLAM AND ARAB QUARTER★★

A precinct with colourful charm and a picture-perfect setting, Kampong Glam is the heart of the island's Malay community. The Sultan Mosque is one of the most photographed tourist landmarks, the Istana Kampong Glam (Malay Heritage Centre) was Singapore's first palace, and the maze of streets surrounding the area claims some of Singapore's coolest fashion shops residing cheek-to-cheek with biryani restaurants, coffee shops and hazy hookah establishments. The area is bordered roughly by Rochor Road, Rochor Canal and Beach Road.

### Walking Tour

*Follow the green line on the map to take this 2.5mi/4km round trip. Allow 3–4hrs to fully experience the sights and shops. Start at the Bugis MRT station.*

#### Bugis Street★

*See SHOPPING.*

From the 1950s to the mid-80s, Bugis Street was a prime attraction of Singapore, known throughout Asia as a red light district where punters, like the Bugis of old, gathered to drink and carouse until the early hours of the morning. A mid-1980s clean-up effort resulted in a complete transformation.
What is now branded "Bugis Street" with a large illuminated sign (a covered melee of shops and food stands) is actually **New Bugis Street**, the result of '80s redevelopment. The original Bugis Street lies opposite, in the **Bugis Junction** mall.

**Touring Tip**

Friday mornings are not a good time to visit this predominantly Muslim area. The shops open late, so come here in the afternoon rather than in the morning. Don't miss the Sultan Mosque or Bussorah Street.

*Sweets at a Bugis Street stall*

J. Gilbert/Michelin

#### Parkview Square

*600 North Bridge Road. Piano bar open daily 11am–midnight. All other floors closed.*

Easily one of the most expensive office buildings in Singapore, the Parkview is also one of the most interesting. Completed in 2002 the building sports a mock Art Deco style (with gargoyles). Visitors are permitted in the outdoor plaza, which is flanked by bronze statues of world figures from politics, the arts and sciences. Stop for a drink in the spacious first-floor **piano bar** with its 15m/49ft ceiling.
*Ophir Road marks the beginning of the Arab Kampong. To your right you will pass Bali and Haji Lane.*

#### Haji Lane

*See SHOPPING.*

In 2006 **Comme des Garçons** opened a retail outlet at number 47 and started a fashion revolution

*Bussorah Street's crafts and antiques shophouses*

J. Gilbert/Michelin

that converted this narrow, quaint street into the hangout of Singapore's trendy crowd. Small boutiques of independent designers mix with second-hand record shops and non-alcoholic cocktail bars.

### Sultan Mosque★★

*3 Muscat Street. Open Sat–Thu 9am–12.45pm & 2pm–4pm, Fri 2.30pm–4pm. 6293 4405.*

The Sultan Mosque is the most important Islamic place of worship in Singapore. From 1824 to 1828, aided by a donation from the East India Company, Sultan Hussein built an Indonesian style mosque, which proved too small for the burgeoning Muslim population. In 1914 a trust was set up to enlarge the mosque. Trustees were members from all Muslim ethnic groups (Arab, Malay, Bugis, Javanese, North Indian and Tamil), which is why Sultan Mosque is considered **Singapore's National Mosque**. The current building (1928) sports a golden onion dome and has a Saracen/Indian appearance. Inside, in the prayer hall, the large **carpet** covering more than 4 000sq m/43 000sq ft is a 1968 Saudi donation, and the **chandeliers** are of similar design to the ones hanging in the Grand Mosque in Mecca.

### Bussorah Street★★

The silhouette of Sultan Mosque's golden dome seems inseparable from its palm-flanked front alley that is Bussorah Street, where shophouses face each other across a pedestrian lane. Like **Kandahar Street** nearby, this street is one of Singapore's most photogenic

**What's in a Name?**

Kampong Glam was the historic seat of Malay royalty in Singapore, dating from the original treaty with Raffles. The name of this *kampong* (village) refers to its original residents, the *orang gelam,* who made a living out of the aromatic *cajeput* oil of the **gelam tree** (*Melaleuca leucadendron*). This tree is a woody perennial that used to grow in the area, belonging to the same family as the better-known Australian Tea Tree, from which the famous oil is extracted.

**Best of Bussorah Street**

Sit outside at **Sleepy Sam's** at #56, a Western café that looks as if it has been transported from Katmandu c.1975, or browse in **Grandfather's Store** at #42, an antiques shop whose window display provides a lesson in the games *kampong* children used to play in these very streets not so long ago.

corners, attracting scores of strolling tourists and busloads of visitors.

### Malay Heritage Centre★

*85 Sultan Gate. Museum open Mon 1pm–6pm, Tue–Sun 10am–6pm. S$4. Gardens 8am–9pm. 6391 0450. www.malayheritage.org.sg.*

This is the original royal residence of the Sultans of Johore, the **Istana Kampong Glam**. Dating from 1840, it was ceded to the sultan and his family, but reverted to Crown property in 1897, as there was no direct descendant of the sultan living there any more. Currently housing the Malay Heritage Centre, it comprises a museum in the Istana itself, a garden and traditional workshops that range from pottery to batik fabrics and music instrumentation. The garden's main attractions are a small-scale replica of a **Bugis fishing boat★** or *prahu*, and a specimen of a **gelam tree**. The museum's more interesting artefacts are on the first floor and include a **tepak sireh** (a betel nut chewing set) and a **Royal Nekara drum★**, whose sound used to accompany the coronation of a

*Saracen-style Sultan Mosque*

J. Gilbert/Michelin

DISTRICTS

Colonial carriage at Malay Heritage Centre

J. Gilbert/Michelin

sultan. The second floor presents contemporary aspects of Malay life in Singapore. The highlight, however, is a complete reconstruction of a **kampong house★**.

*Gedung Kuning/Tepak Sireh 73 Sultan Gate. Open Mon–Sat 12pm–2.30pm, 3pm–5.30pm & 6.30pm–10pm. 6396 4373/6291 2873. www.gedungkuning.com/ www.tepaksireh.com.sg.*

The **Gedung Kuning** (Yellow Mansion) made of wood and bricks but plastered to a Palladian finish, was part of the Sultan's Palace compound from the 1860s onwards. Currently, it houses the Malay restaurant **Tepak Sireh**. Hours given above are for lunch, tea and dinner respectively.

### Hajjah Fatimah Mosque★

*4001 Beach Road. Open Sat–Thu 9am–1pm & 2pm-4pm, Fri 2.30pm–4pm. 6297 2774.*

Hajjah Fatimah was the Malaccan wife of the wealthy Bugis Sultan of Gowa, who lived on the site where the current mosque stands. In the 1830s the house was deliberately set on fire, but she was away at the time; Fatimah, by now a widow, subsequently designated the land for a mosque to express her gratitude for her survival. The mosque was completed in 1846 in a mix of styles, with European Doric columns, a Malay minaret and an Arab dome. Its minaret is optimistically called the **"Leaning Tower of Singapore"**, because of its six-degree incline to the horizontal, a design feature rather than the effect of subsidence.

### Malabar, or Blue Mosque★

*471 Victoria Street. Open Sat–Thu 6am–10:30pm except during prayers. 6294 3862.*

Completed in 1963, this mosque is managed by and for the Malabar community of South India and is not open for tourism purposes. With its small hexagonal tiles in various shades of blue, it strikes a handsome presence on Victoria Street. Behind it is a **Muslim cemetery★** dating from 1819 and overgrown with vegetation.

# ORCHARD ROAD★★

Ask a Singaporean which street best epitomises their city—and most will reply Orchard Road: a tree-lined one-way street stretching 2.5km/1.5mi, crammed with around 20 steel, glass or concrete **shopping malls** (and always with more on the way). Plasma screens play glamourous adverts to those who wait to cross by the lights (no jaywalking here), a sudden blast of air-conditioning cools you down as you walk past a mall entrance, and there's always a feeling that if you aren't already shopping, you should be. Singapore's relentless, crowded, vibrant shopping hub is the main drag up from the **Colonial District** to the **Botanic Gardens**, and stretches from Dhoby Ghaut at its eastern end, to Tanglin in the west. *For a description of individual shops on and near Orchard Road, see SHOPPING.*

## Dhoby Ghaut Area

At the eastern end of Orchard Road, Dhoby Ghaut's famous landmark is the **Istana**, residence of Singapore's president, with its vast, verdant grounds. Nearby at Oxley Rise and Tank Road, attractions encapsulate Singapore's multicultural identity, including Judaism, Christianity, Hinduism, Chinese clans and Confucius worship. Step back from the dazzling malls for some real gems.

## Walking Tour

*Follow the blue line on the map. Tour takes about 3hrs (3–4km/1.8–2.5mi). Exit the MRT at Dhoby Ghaut. Start at House of Tan Yeok Nee.*

Not advisable midday, this walk is ideal in the late afternoon, when most places are still open.

### House of Tan Yeok Nee

*101 Penang Road. Open Mon–Fri 9.30am–5pm. Although unofficially, the security guard inside the main entrance may show you around, unless classes or events. 6238 2193.*

Built by a wealthy merchant in the late 19C, this structure is now a branch of the University of Chicago Graduate School. If entry is not possible, wander around the outside to see the ornately carved roof. The last of four great 19C Teow Chew buildings, the design

Orchard Road

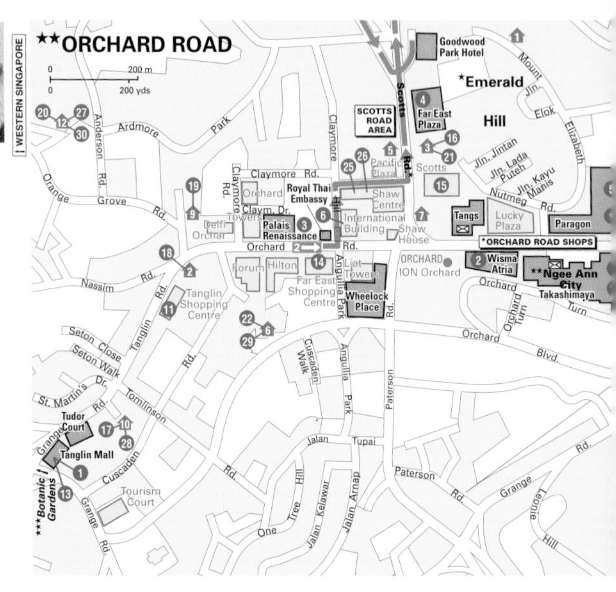


is a typical Chinese style. If you get to see inside, look for the carved **marble pillars** relating to the merchant's ancestors, the tiled beams and gold-plate carvings.

**Istana Park**

*Between Orchard and Penang Roads and Penang Lane. Open daily 24hrs. Changing of the Guard on last Sun of every month, 6pm.*

Unless you come on a public holiday (with a rare opening of the **Istana**), relax in the shady park at the lotus pond, or the elegant Palm Pool with its contemporary steel sculpture **Festival Arch**. A little-used oasis by day, the park is the best vantage point for the monthly **Changing of the Guard** at the Istana Gateway opposite. British-style pageantry uses 38

Green space adjoining Istana Park

J. Gilbert/Michelin

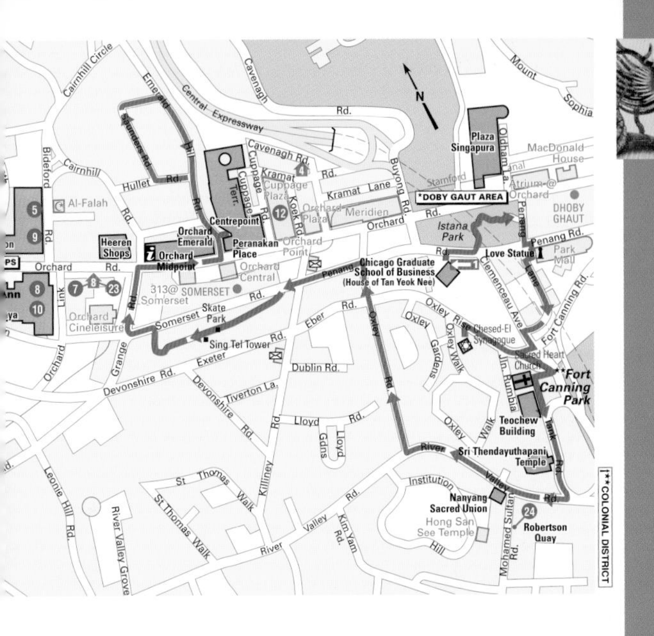

**Hotels**

1. The Elizabeth Hotel
2. Orchard Parade Hotel
3. Grand Hyatt
4. Holiday Inn Park View
5. Royal Plaza on Scotts
6. Four Seasons
7. Marriott
8. Meritus Mandarin
9. Orchard Hotel
10. The Regent
11. The Shangri-La

**Restaurants**

1. Caffe Beviamo
2. Food Republic
3. Marmalade Pantry
4. Pondok Jawa Timur
5. Thai Express
6. The Rice Table
7. Chatterbox
8. Crystal Jade Palace
9. Din Tai Fung
10. Imperial Treasure Nan Bei
11. Indian Grill
12. Kazu Sumiyaki
13. Patara
14. Shashlik
15. Soup Restaurant
16. Straits Kitchen
17. Summer Palace
18. Club Chinois
19. Hua Ting
20. The Line
21. Mezza9
22. One-Ninety
23. Pine Court
24. Sage
25. La Strada
26. Les Amis
27. Blu
28. Iggy's
29. Jiang Nan Chun
30. Nadaman

**What's the Meaning of This?**

In early Singapore, Orchard Road's eastern end was an open-air laundry, owned by early Indian immigrants. The *dhobies* (Hindi word for laundrymen; *ghaut* or *ghat* means river bank) washed the locals' laundry in the stream, now the Stamford Canal, drying it on the surrounding green lawns. Until the early 1970s there were a few traditional shophouses, plus the Cathay Building, which in 1939 was Singapore's first skyscraper and air-conditioned public space. This area was also the location of the Jewish Cemetery, until everything changed with the building of the MRT.

guards in strict formation with rifle precision drill performances to please the crowd. At the entrance are nibong trees and a mangrove palm.

### Chesed-El Synagogue

*Oxley Rise. Enquire at Maghain Aboth Synagogue about hours and services. 6337 2189.*

Although the building and gates are usually closed, wander around the outside of this dramatic white synagogue, built in 1905 in the Palladian style. Its Iraqi-born founder was a generous and controversial member of the Jewish community, then based at Maghain Aboth synagogue on Waterloo Street. After World War II the Singapore government wanted to take over the property—even though the synagogue still owns the land. To retain it, the community decided to keep it open once a week.

**Light Bites**

**Crossroads Cafe** – *http://crossroads.singaporemarriott.com.*
A perfect spot for a break from shopping with a cold beer, light lunch or hearty plate of noodles. Ideally located at the corner of Scotts and Orchard roads, with open doors onto the street.

J. Gilbert/Michelin

**Cable Car** – This loosely themed 1890s saloon is moments away from Orchard Road and a rare chance for an alfresco beer or bar snacks.

**Jackie Chan's Cafe** – The action movie megastar opened this bright informal café in 2007, good for a mug of coffee, soup and dim sum on the sofa. If you're inspired by footage of Chan's achievements on the plasma screen, there are T-shirts for sale. Keep a look out, he sometimes drops in for a cup of his favourite Mi Xiang Pu Er tea.

**The Dubliner** – *165 Penang Road. www.dublinersingapore.com.*
Take time out from sightseeing to sample some pub food in this traditional Irish bar. While you're here, admire the architecture of the restored Colonial house it occupies. *See NIGHTLIFE.*

### Istana and the President

The president's residence, Government House, is a classical bungalow in the neo-Palladian style with graceful arches, built in 1869 by Indian convict labour. Covering 40ha/100 acres, it was renamed Istana Negara (Malay for palace) in 1959 when Singapore gained independence. The grounds, once a nutmeg estate, now contain 100-year-old tembusu trees, foxtail palms, Swan Pond, lizards and bats. Although presidents usually reside here, current President SR Nathan chooses to reside in his more modest home in Singapore's outskirts. Holding a position more akin to a ceremonial head of state, Nathan was first elected in 1999, then re-elected in 2005 and stands to stay in power until 2011. The entire grounds are opened to the public five days a year: Chinese New Year, Deepavali, Hari Raya Puasa, Labour Day and National Day.

## Sacred Heart Church

*111 Tank Road. Open 7am–7pm daily. Mass daily. 6737 9285.*

Two small marble lions stand guard at the main gate of this Catholic church, built in 1910 to serve the Hakka and Cantonese-speaking community. Designed in the French Baroque style, the two side altars are made from French-imported white marble carved by French stonemasons, and the pews from chengal wood, made by Bangkok craftsmen.

## Teochew Building

*97 Tank Road. Open daily 10am–6pm. 6737 9555. www.ngeeann.com.sg.*

This distinctive pagoda-style building archives historical items of the Teochew clan from China. The small Level 2 exhibit includes the history of wealthy merchants who came to Singapore in the mid-19C and assisted their fellow Teochews. Watch for the intricate **model** of today's vast mall Ngee Ann City, which lies on land originally bought from the East India Company for 649 Indian Rupees.

## Sri Thendayuthapani Temple

*15 Tank Road. Open daily 8am–12pm and 5.30pm–8.30pm (worship). Fee may be charged if you take photos. 6737 9393. www.sttemple.com.*

Honouring Lord Thendayuthapani, this temple is also known as Chettiars' Temple after the south Indian moneylending caste who built it in 1859. Its ornate exterior has sculptures of Hindu gods at the entrance. A cool green interior shows off pillars, shrines and etched-glass ceiling panels. Busy evenings see devotees offer coconuts, bananas and even cartons of milk at the garlanded shrines of Hindu gods. The annual Thaipusam festival *(Jan/Feb)* attracts thousands for prayer and processions (*see CALENDAR OF EVENTS*).

### Touring Tip

Late afternoon or early evening is the most comfortable time to visit, but come armed with insect repellent. There's a visitor centre on Orchard Road, near the junction of Cairnhill Road *(take Somerset MRT and exit left).*

### Nanyang Sacred Union

*231–235 River Valley Road. Open daily 9am–5pm.*

Enter through the gate (ring the bell) at this small Chinese temple with a richly carved roof. Originally a mid-19C mansion, it converted to a temple in the 1930s. There are separate worship rooms for Taoism, Confucianism and Buddhism, but the highlight is the **central hall**, for the worship of Confucius, with the painted portrait and principles of the philosopher as focal points. Locals place paper money in the courtyard's furnaces for their loved ones to enjoy in the afterlife. There are places where you can pop in for lunch or a pint before continuing down Penang Road. Cross Killiney Road and walk along the grass, with the huge **SingTel Tower** on your left. Graffiti (unusual in Singapore) marks the **Skate Park**, where young Singaporeans skateboard on some of the city's most valuable real estate.

*Emerald Hill houses, Orchard Road mall in background*

J. Gilbert/Michelin

*Emerald Hill's artsy feel*

J. Gilbert/Michelin

### Emerald Hill★

End your walk with a quiet stroll past this enclave of handsome terraces (now home to chic bars and restaurants) that once belonged to wealthy Straits Chinese (known as Peranakans). At the bottom of the hill is **Peranakan Corner**, built in 1902 and redeveloped for S$2.2 million, forming the gateway to Emerald Hill Conservation Area. **No. 56** marks one of the earliest terraces built in the Transitional Style, with three French windows on level 2. **No. 45** is everyone's dream house, with a grand frontage and ornate Chinese tiles over the forecourt wall. The Art-Deco-style **nos. 121-129** have simple fanlights and none of the previously seen plaster moulding. Reward yourself with a cool drink at the hip **Alley Bar** *(see NIGHTLIFE)*, in one of several restored houses. The walls of the VIP room are lined with fascinating black-and-white photographs of Peranakan families who lived in this area.

## Scotts Road Area

Leafy Scotts Road runs north off the western end of Orchard Road, with Tang's distinctive pagoda as your landmark. The looping Goodwood Hill has Singapore's largest intact collection of Colonial black-and-white houses built in the 1920s, a period of rapid suburban growth.

## The Life Colonial

### Royal Thai Embassy

*370 Orchard Rd.*

Originally known as the **Hurricane House**, it was bought by King Chulalongkorn of Siam after his first visit here in 1871 (then age 18). The house is now the venue of the embassy, with lush gardens.

### Scotts Road Bungalows

*From 29 Scotts Rd. Sporadic hours.*

These four black-and-white bungalows are the last surviving bungalows on Scotts Road. Built in the late 1920s, the luxury houses represent Singapore's post-war boom. Typically, the residents were middle-class Asians and Euro-Asians.

### Goodwood Hill

*Go counterclockwise around the hill.*

This residential area reveals a charming street of black-and-white detached villas, built mainly for senior civil servants in the early 20C. Some reflect the style of mid-19C plantations, with wooden verandas and timber columns on all sides. Some were built for senior members of the judiciary.

###  Goodwood Park Hotel

*22 Scotts Road. 6737 7411. www.goodwoodparkhotel.com.*

Built as the Teutonia Club in 1900, the hotel has a fairytale castle appearance, with an equally dramatic history. It hosted cultural evenings for the local German community. Bought after World War I and renamed Goodwood Hall, it was a fashionable venue and hotel for many years.
Today the hotel is still one of Singapore's finest *(see HOTELS)*. Goodwood was made a national monument in 1989. Step inside to drink a toast to its history and enjoy an English high tea.

Goodwood Park Hotel

J. Gilbert/Michelin

DISTRICTS

# MUSEUMS

To fully appreciate the cultural diversity of Singapore, a visit to the city-state's museums is a must. The Asian Civilisations Museum is the only place on the continent where the major cultures that make up Singapore (Indian, Muslim, Southeast Asian and Chinese) can be compared side by side. History buffs will want to head to The National Museum for a look at Singapore's past. Art lovers should see the works at the Singapore Art Museum, and stamp collectors will appreciate the Philatelic Museum. Just about everyone should view the exquisite artefacts at the Peranakan Museum.

## Asian Civilisations Museum★★

*See COLONIAL DISTRICT.*
*1 Empress Place. Open Mon 1pm–7pm, Tue–Sun 9am–7pm, Fri 9am–9pm. S$8. Tours in English Mon 2pm, Tue–Fri 11am, 2pm, Sat–Sun 1.30pm. 6332 7798/2982. www.acm.org.sg.*

This fascinating museum provides a close look at the magnificent art and artefacts of India, China, Southeast Asia and the Arab world. Along with The National Museum, it is the successor to the Raffles Library and Museum (1887).

### Southeast Asia: Galleries 3 and 4

In these two vast galleries, highlights from the Hindu/Buddhist early Empires, the Theravada Buddhist Kingdoms of Indo-China, the Javanese Kingdoms, and the Malay world are the **Dong Son★★★** ceremonial bronze drums from North Vietnam (180–100 BC), a seated marble Burmese **Buddha★** and a bronze 5C standing **Buddha★** from Kedah. Tribal artefacts include a **carved shrunken head★★★** from the Dayak in Borneo (c.1900), and the large 1.2kg/2.5lb silver-gold earrings from North Sumatra called **Padung-padung★★**.

Asian Civilisations Museum

*Dong Son drum*

### Islam: Gallery 5

Dated early 8C, the **Kufic-Abbasid Qur'an Folio★★★** written with ink on parchment is one of the earliest examples of Qur'anic verses. Another standout is a gold-leaf Burmese **box★★** for storing the Muslim holy book. Look up to spot the black silken **Kiswah★** (a curtain covering of the Ka'bah in Mecca) with gold-threaded embroidery. Below that, the **Firman of Sultan Abdul Hamid II★★** (1893) is written in a special script that is tightly packed to avoid forgery. Although images are prohibited in Islam, an 11–12C **incense burner★★** from Egypt is shaped like a lion.

**Tips for Your Visit**

Allow 2–4hrs for a visit to the Asian Civilisations Museum. Obtain a map at the entrance; there is a guidebook that you can buy in the bookshop, if you wish. One-hour guided tours concentrate on highlights, but with more than 10 galleries and extensive explanatory notes, the museum is best explored on your own.
The museum begins at Level 2 with the Singapore River Gallery 1 and an Introductory Gallery 2. The more impressive exhibition starts with the Southeast Asia Galleries 3 and 4. Move then to Gallery 5 (Islam) and continue to Gallery 6 (China), and if you don't have time, skip Level 3 and walk straight down to Level 1 for the West Asia/Indian Galleries 7 and 8.

### China: Gallery 6

The Emperor's yellow **Long Pao or Dragon's Robe★** with sewn dragons has 12 imperial symbols from the Qian Long period (1736–95). The star item, though, is the collection of 17C **Dehua figurines★★★** made of *blanc-de-chine* porcelain. The masterpiece is a fine **seated Sakyamuni**, which does not look at all like a Buddha, unshaven and fasting as it is.

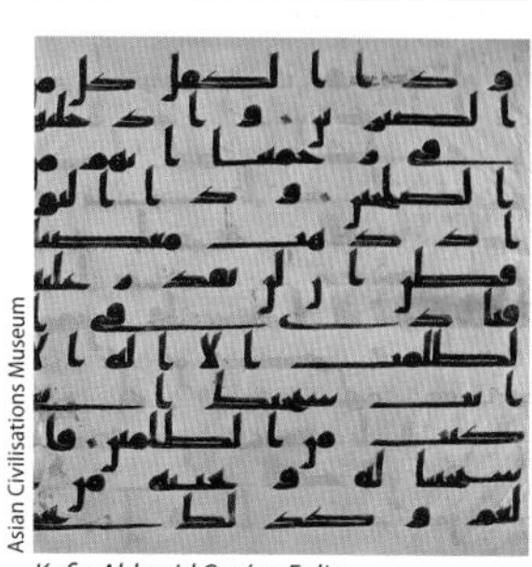

Asian Civilisations Museum

*Kufic-Abbasid Qur'an Folio*

### India: Galleries 7 and 8

On the first floor is a large ornamental **Mughal gateway** (17C) from Vraja. Farther in, the **Chola bronzes★★★** from Tamil Nadu (c.1200) represent Shiva, Parvati and their son Skanda plus Hanuman, the monkey god. A 12C **Nataraja★** (Dancing Shiva) sculpture from Karnataka and a 9C red sandstone **Vishnu idol★★** complete the Hindu pantheon. A **Kushana Buddha★★** from Afghanistan is one of only four in existence.

### Level 3

**Gallery 4a** contains the instruments of an Indonesian **Gamelan** orchestra, plus masks and shadow puppets. The most interesting artefacts in **Gallery**

**Empress Place**

Sporting Doric columns, the austere museum building was designed in the Neo-Palladian style by JFA McNair in the 1860s (with extensions in the 20C). It once held the offices of government, but was renovated as an exhibition hall in the 1980s. In 1993 the Asian Civilisations Museum split from The National Museum and was housed in the Peranakan Museum on Armenian Street. The Empress Place building became the main home of the Asian Civilisations Museum in 2003.

**Tips for Your Visit**

The multimedia guide, free with your ticket to The National Museum, is excellent. Every exhibit has a number and while the commentary goes on, you can type in this number to see a detailed description of the exhibit on the screen. The complete material contained in the guide is on the order of eight hours. Budget a minimum 2 hours for your visit – 3 if you also wish to see the Lifestyle section (the Living Galleries).

**5a** are Sufi music paraphernalia and an old **astrolab★** used in navigation by Arab traders.

## The National Museum★★

*See COLONIAL DISTRICT. 93 Stamford Road. Singapore History Gallery open daily 10am–6pm, Singapore Living Galleries open daily 10am–8pm (free 6pm–8pm). S$10. One-hour tours Mon–Fri 11am, 2pm, Sat–Sun 11.30am, 2pm, 3.30pm. 6332 3659/5642. www.nationalmuseum.sg.*

The oldest museum in Singapore, the National is divided into the main History Gallery, which traces the story of Singapore from the 14C to the present, and the less visited Living Galleries, which illustrates the lives of the people of Singapore through the years. The latter galleries are structured around four themes: **Fashion**, **Food**, **Photography** and **Film**. Opened in 1887 to celebrate Queen Victoria's Gold Jubilee, the building originally housed the **Raffles Library and Museum**, whose primary focus was natural history and anthropology.

*Portrait of Sir Frank Athelstane Swettenham (1904) by John Singer Sargent*

National Museum of Singapore

### History Gallery

The first exhibit spotlights the **Singapore Stone★★★**(10C–14C), a fragment of a 3m/10ft high, 3m/10ft long boulder with ancient inscriptions. Found at the entrance of the Singapore river near the present-day Fullerton Hotel, it was blown up in 1819 during the clearing of the jungle. It remains one of the biggest unsolved archaeological mysteries, as no one has been able to decipher it or assign it to a specific civilisation. The current thinking is that it is a variant of old Sumatran script and possibly a marker of the ancient Srivijayan Empire (4C–12C).

In the first room, gold **Majapahit ornaments★★** from the 1928 excavations at Fort Canning date to the 14C. In the next room, a **daguerreotype of Singapore** (1844) shows the view from present-day Fort Canning. The **portrait**

Xin Sai Le Puppet Stage

National Museum of Singapore

**of Raffles** by George Joseph is the best-known likeness of Raffles. The most imposing item in the museum is the **funeral hearse of Tan Jiak Kim★★** (1917), made of wood lacquer and iron.
The museum's most valuable artefact is **John Singer Sargent's** 1904 painting of **Sir Frank Athelstane Swettenham★★**.
Designed by Chinese artists, the **natural history watercolours★** combine Oriental techniques with the aesthetics of Western art. The **golden mace★** was presented to the city to commemorate the granting of a royal charter by King George VI, who raised the status of Singapore to a city in 1951.

### Living Galleries

These galleries are of limited interest to the general visitor. What should not be missed, however, is the Fashion Gallery's wooden **puppet stage★★** belonging to the Xin Sai Le troupe from Fujian in the 1930s. Lit by more than 1 000 light bulbs, it measures 4.4m/14.5ft in width and 1.9m/6.2ft in height and comes with 45 puppets, 96 costumes, 56 hats, 24 pieces of backdrops and 20 props pieces that were kept in two wooden chests.

## Chinatown Heritage Centre★

Although this centre is not formally a museum, it provides an invaluable look at the lives of the early Chinese in Singapore through artefacts, photographs, a model junk and re-created rooms. *For description, see CHINATOWN.*

## Peranakan Museum★

*See COLONIAL DISTRICT.*
*39 Armenian Street. Open Mon 1pm–7pm, Tue–Thu, Sat–Sun 9.30am–7pm, Fri 9.30am–9pm. S$6. 6332 7591. www.peranakanmuseum.sg.*

One of Singapore's most spectacular museums is housed in the old **Tao Nan** school building founded in 1906 by the **Hokkien Association**. Originally teaching in Hokkien, it was the first school to start instructing in the new unifying language, **Mandarin**, in 1916. The building was the seat of the Asian Civilisations Museum before it moved to its present Empress Place site—minus the Peranakan (Straits-born Chinese) artefacts that are accommodated here at the Peranakan Museum. On view are exquisite displays of intricately crafted jewellery, gold and silver ornaments, textiles, ceramics and furniture in ten permanent galleries. Look out for the traditional wedding procession, the **wedding bed** gilded with fertility symbols, the 16-piece floral porcelain dinner set and the monumental ancestral altar.

Singapore Philatelic Museum

J. Gilbert/Michelin

## Singapore Philatelic Museum★

*See COLONIAL DISTRICT.*
*23B Coleman Street. Open Mon 1pm–7pm, Tue–Sun 9am–7pm. S$5. 6337 3888. www.spm.org.sg.*

Dating from 1906, this building sports a handsome façade with arched verandas and ornamental transom windows above the main doors. It was part of the Anglo-Chinese school, and was later used as a Methodist bookshop until the establishment of the Philatelic Museum in August 1995.
On the second floor there is a permanent exhibit comprising an introduction to philately and stamp design, as well as a Room of Rarities (including a Penny Black) and a Heritage Room. Temporary exhibits are also on display. The museum's biggest claim to fame, nevertheless, must be the complete collection of **Harry Potter stamps** from around the world.

## Singapore Art Museum

*See COLONIAL DISTRICT.*
*71 Bras Basah Road. Open Mon–Sun 10am–7pm (Fri til 9pm). S$8 (S$10 both museums). Tours Mon 2pm, Tue–Thu 11am, 2pm, Fri 11am, 2pm, 7pm, Sat, Sun 11am, 2pm, 3.30pm. 6332 3222. www.singart.com.*

The museum occupies the former grounds of **St. Joseph's Institute**, a Catholic school for boys established in 1852. The present building dates from 1867. In 1987 the school was relocated, and in 1996 the art museum was officially opened. From 2001, it began acquiring works and accepting donations from around the Southeast Asia region. In mid-2008 the museum opened **8Q sam**, an art space devoted to new media and contemporary works

Singapore Art Museum

J. Gilbert/Michelin

of living artists. Also housed in a former school building, 8Q sam sits around the corner at 8 Queen Street. Numbering over 6 500 pieces, the museum's permanent collection, exhibited on rotation every three to six months, contains works by contemporary Singaporean and Southeast Asian artists. Among these artists are **Georgette Chen** (1907–92), who trained in Paris and is considered to be a pioneer of the "Nanyang" style; **Chen Chong Swee** (1910–1985), who was a major influence in the development of Singaporen art; and social realist **Chua Mia Tee** (b.1931), who attended the Nanyang Academy of Fine Arts. More recent work is represented by **Lim Tze Peng**, a Cultural Medallion winner (2003).

## Fuk Tak Chi Museum

*See CHINATOWN.*
*76 Telok Ayer Street. Open daily 10am–10pm. 6532 7868.*

This small building, comprising only a court and a shrine room, was the first Chinese temple in Singapore. Erected c.1824, soon after Raffles laid out his plans for the island, it stood on the shore where Chinese immigrants landed. It was dedicated to Tua Pek Kong, the god (usually depicted as a smiling old man with a white beard) who gave protection against illness and danger. In the 1990s the temple moved to a shrine in Geylang, while this historic building was redeveloped into a museum and re-opened to the public in 1998. The museum is the city's first street museum. It has amassed more than 2 000 artefacts over the years from Chinatown residents.

A glass case contains a **model** of Telok Ayer Street's appearance in the mid-1800s when the majority of Chinese immigrants arrived.

## Changi Chapel & Museum★

*In Eastern Singapore.*
*1000 Upper Changi Road North. Open daily 9.30am–5pm (last admission 4.30pm). Guided tour (45–60min) S$8. 6214 2451. www.changimuseum.com.*
*By car: From city area, head for Pan Island Expressway and take the exit towards TPE/SLE. By bus or MRT: Take SBS Bus No. 2 from Tanah Merah MRT Station or SBS Bus No. 29 from Tampines MRT Station. Alight at the Changi Museum bus stop.*

Changi is located on the extreme eastern end of Singapore, extending to Loyang Avenue and Changi Coast Road. During World War II, the Japanese set up prisoners-of-war camps in Changi. The exhibits in the Changi Chapel & Museum are the only clues to this area's tragic history.

The entrance gallery provides an overview of life in Changi before **World War II** and the changes brought about by militarization. On display are personal effects and artefacts along with stories of the experiences and sufferings of the Allied prisoners of war (mostly Australians and British) during World War II. One of them was James Clavell, who would go on to pen the book *King Rat,* which was based on his experiences in the prison. Impressive exhibits include re-creations of the **Changi Murals** by war veteran Bombardier Stanley Warren, and the simple, wooden **Changi Prison Chapel**.

# PARKS, GARDENS AND RESERVES

For a city that has so much steel and concrete, Singapore has a surprisingly large number of places where nature thrives, with myriad plant and bird life. Singapore Botanic Gardens in the Orchard Road area is an urban oasis within the city centre, while four **nature reserves** lie farther afield. All offer visitors respite, beauty and discovery.

## Singapore Botanic Gardens★★★

*1 Cluny Road, 1.5km/.9mi from the western end of Orchard Road, accessible via Tanglin and Napier Roads. Buses run on Orchard Boulevard to Tanglin Gate. Open daily 5am–midnight. Tours available most Sat. 6471 7361. www.sbg.org.sg.*

These gardens encompass 640 000 sq m/765 500sq yds, with blissful pathways through 2 000 varieties of flora, including the outstanding National Orchid Garden. Founded in 1859, the gardens were originally ornamental, yet quickly evolved into a horticultural hub assisted by botanists trained at London's Kew Gardens. In 1888 the first director, **Henry Nicholas Ridley**, developed a foolproof way to tap rubber trees, and turned the gardens into a plantation. As the auto industry boomed in the early 1900s, the gardens gained an invaluable source of income.

At the Viewing Terrace, visitors can watch Tai Chi Chuan exercises, usually until around 10am

**Touring Tip**

Mornings or late afternoons are usually the most comfortable in terms of temperature. Allow 2–3 hours to explore the whole gardens. If you have only an hour, head for the National Orchid Garden. First pick up a map and bottle of water at the visitor centre. Start in the garden's central area, and if time, head to the western then to the eastern section and **Jacob Ballas Children's Garden.**

*National Orchid Garden*



MUST SEE

National flower: Vanda Miss Joaquim

J. Gilbert/Michelin

**Singapore's National Flower**

In 1893 while tending her garden, **Agnes Joaquim** spotted a new hybrid of orchid, and rushed to Henry Ridley, then Director of the Botanic Gardens, for his expertise. Previously unknown to science, it prompted the creation of new laboratories for orchid breeding and hybridisation. Thus began a multimillion dollar cut-flower industry, putting Singapore's orchid hybrids firmly on the world map.

In 1981 the hybrid of *Vanda hookeriana* and *Vanda teres* – named after Ms. Joaquim – became Singapore's official flower, known for its year-round hardy purple blooms.

*(visitors welcome; loose clothing recommended).* Covered by a canopy of trees, the **Rainforest Path** is one of Singapore's only areas of original jungle, with 314 species of vegetation. The tallest trees are a mammoth 40m/131ft high. The Orchid Plaza serves as the entrance to the splendid **National Orchid Garden** *(open daily 8.30am–7pm; S$5),* the world's largest display of orchids—some 1 000 species and 2 000 hybrids. From the Crane Fountain, meandering paths lead to the VIP Orchid Garden. Here you can see hybrids named after prominent people, from esteemed biochemists to Princess Diana (delicate white and pink blooms). The display in Holttum Hall, location of the original orchid seedling culture lab, details the science of developing the perfect hybrid. Back in the Botanic Gardens, take the elevated walkway to cool down in the Cool House, which re-creates a tropical mountain forest complete with ferns, moss and unusual orchid species. Walk from Orchid Plaza along Lower Palm Valley Road to **Symphony Lake**, the garden's smallest artificial lake with lotus flowers and fish. The **Shaw Foundation Symphony Stage** is built on an islet near its southern tip, and hosts the occasional evening concert by the Singapore Symphony Orchestra. Circle the lake, looking out for **EJH Corner** to the southwest, a bungalow named after Corner, assistant director, 1929–1945. From here, walk east via the the **Evolution Garden** to **Eco Lake**. Or explore the western section, with **Swan Lake** and the Victorian **Bandstand**.

## Night Safari★★★

*In Northern Singapore. 80 Mandai Lake Road. Open daily 7.30pm–midnight. S$22. Tram tours S$10. 6269 3411. www.nightsafari.com.sg. Take Pan Island Expressway toward Jurong to Exit 7 for Bukit Timah Expressway and follow signs. See the website for public and private (door-to-door) bus service.*

Located next to the Singapore Zoo *(see FOR KIDS)*, Night Safari is the world's first wildlife park built for nocturnal visits. As 90 percent of

tropical animals are more active after dark, the best time to see them is at night. Only open after dark, the park takes advantage of the regularity of sunset at 7.30pm in equatorial Singapore and the island's cool, dry nights. Everything is done to give the impression that visitors are exploring a jungle at night. Subtle lighting illuminates without disturbing the 100-plus species in their natural habitat. Several walkable trails include the **Bat Mangrove Walk** inhabited by Malayan bats, and the **Leopard Trail** where you might see the clouded leopard, Asian bearcat and Malayan civet. The highlight, however, is the 45-minute **tram ride** with live commentary across a landscape ranging from Himalayan foothills (tahr, bharal and vultures) and a Nepalese river valley (otter, wolf, greater Asian rhino and jackal) to the Indian subcontinent (striped hyena, lion and sloth bear). The tram stops at the "Creatures of the Night Show", which focuses on the nocturnal activites of the puma, barn owl, python and raccoon. Visitors then get back on board for an "overnight" trip to Equatorial Africa, featuring giraffe, serval, spotted hyena and hippo. The ride ends back at the **Indo-Malayan region** that is home to the nocturnal hog deer, bearded pig and Malayan tiger. Cultural presentations include tribal dances and tribal skills.

**Taxi Tip**

Taxis are the easiest way to get to most parks and reserves, but avoid peak travel times *(Mon–Fri 7am–9.30am and 5pm–8pm)* when traffic and ERP toll charges (Electronic Road Pricing) hike up the meter.

###  Mandai Orchid Garden★★

*200 Mandai Lake Road. Open Mon 8am–6pm, Tue–Sun 8am–7pm. S$3.50. 6269 1036.*

Located near Night Safari, this garden should be visited in daylight before heading to the neighbouring wildlife park. Although the Singapore Botanic Gardens have a better offering, the 200-plus orchid varieties here, together with herbs, spices and fruits, are worth a look in tandem with your visit to Night Safari. With all these orchids, exotic birds like the Little Spiderhunter and the Purple-throated Sunbird are attracted to the gardens.

## Central Catchment Nature Reserve★★

Made up of the Upper and Lower Seletar, Bukit Timah and MacRitchie reservoirs, the Central Catchment is a paradise for nature lovers and photographers. Lying north of Singapore City, the area is bounded by Lornie Road, Upper Thomson Road, Bukit Timah Expressway and Seletar Expressway. Some 840 flowering plants and 500 species of animals are found in the Bukit Timah and Central Catchment reserves, with new species being recorded each year. To develop Singapore as a trading port, forests were cleared and by 1886, only 10 percent of the original forest remained. The rapid destruction was halted when the MacRitchie Reservoir was developed. Surrounding forest was preserved as a water catchment area. For more

Long-tailed macaque, MacRitchie Reservoir Park

J. Gilbert/Michelin

information, contact the Bukit Timah Nature Reserve Visitor Centre *(177 Hindhede Drive; 6468 5736; www.nparks.gov.sg)*.

### MacRitchie Reservoir Park★

*Off Lornie Road. From the city, head for Bukit Timah Road. Then stay on Thomson Road. After a slight left at Lornie Road, make a U-turn. Then turn onto Reservoir Road. For public bus service: www.nparks.gov.sg. Park open daily. HSBC Tree Top Walk open Tue–Fri 9am–5pm, Sat, Sun and public holidays 8.30am–5pm.*

Around the reservoir are remnants of primary forest, swamps and the plantations that once flourished here. Besides rubber and chestnut trees, giant trees like the Jelutong and Seraya are typical of the lowland forests. Several trails wend their way through the jungle and around the lakeshore,

**HSBC Tree Top Walk**

The HSBC-sponsored 250m/820ft treetop suspension bridge was created to observe the canopy of the rain forest and is a great opportunity for natural history enthusiasts to see life at the top of the trees. The full trail, of which the bridge is only a part, is 11km/6.8mi long from the park entrance. On the treetop walkway there is a one-way system so that the bridge does not suffer from traffic jams. The walkway is some 25m/82ft from the forest floor at its highest point. The numbers on the walkway are controlled and groups of 30 are the limit at any one time.

There are two rest stops at 2.8km/1.75mi and 5km/3mi. The full walk can be tiring in the heat, so bring plenty of bottled water. Keep all foodstuffs in a bag or backpack and try not to eat in view of any monkeys, as they are pesky and clever food thieves. The Ranger Station has toilets, a water cooler and an information kiosk. To date the research that has taken place *(on Mondays when the walkway is closed)* has discovered 80 varieties of bird life including the **Drongo Cuckoo**, the **Thick Billed Green Pigeon** and **Green Leafbirds**. From the reptile kingdom comes the **Black Bearded Dragon** and the **Clouded Monitor**.

some of them on boardwalks. One trail takes you to the **HSBC Tree Top Walk** *(see box below)* above the forest canopy along a suspension bridge that is situated between the two highest points in MacRitchie.

### Bukit Timah Nature Reserve★★

*177 Hindhede Drive. From the city, head for Bukit Timah Road. Turn right at Jalan Anak Bukit. Continue onto Upper Bukit Timah Road and make a U-turn for Hindhede Road. Make a slight right for Hindhede Drive. Reserve open daily 6am–7pm.*

The reserve is home to Singapore's highest peak, **Bukit Timah Hill**, which stands at 164m/538ft above sea level. It is one of the few places left with primary rain forest cover. The area was once the home of tigers, some of which were man-eaters, but sadly they have all been wiped out. Most commonly seen animals are long-tailed macaques and flying lemurs. Common tree shrews and plantain squirrels can also be seen.

### Pierce Reservoir Park

*Lower Pierce is located off Upper Thomson Road. From the city, head to Bukit Timah Road. Then stay on Thomson Road. Take the exit toward Upper Thomson Road. Make a slight left at Old Upper Thomson Road, and make a left again. For public bus service: www.nparks.gov.sg. Park open daily.*

Lower Pierce has a 900m/985yd boardwalk through a secondary forest filled with century-old trees. Watch out for Upper Pierce's fierce monkeys that sometimes mug passers-by for food. The 6ha/15acre park is perfect for a family outing or picnic. Most of the forest seen in Upper Pierce used to be gambier and pepper plantations in the late 19C.

### Seletar Reservoir Park

*Bounded by Yishun Avenue 1 and Lentor Avenue. From the city, take Bukit Timah Road and later, the CLE. After it merges onto the SLE, head for the exit for Upper Thompson Road. Turn left at Mandai Road, then turn left at Mandai Road 7. For public bus service: www.nparks.gov.sg. Park open daily and lit 7pm–7am.*

Situated on the northern shore of Lower Seletar Reservoir, this parkland is largely flat with some undulating terrain that provides a pleasant place for a leisurely stroll or a jog. Benches line the reservoir for those preferring to sit back and enjoy the calm waters of the reservoir.

## Jurong Bird Park★★

*2 Jurong Hill. From the city, take the ECP, then the AYE. Take the exit towards Jurong island; merge onto Jalan Ahmad Ibrahim. Turn left at Bird Park Drive. Turn right towards Jurong Hill and turn left at Jurong Hill. Or take the MRT to Boon Lay Station and transfer to SBS 194 or 251 at the Boon Lay Bus Interchange. Open daily 8.30am–6pm. S$18, S$9 children. 6265 0022. www.birdpark.com.sg.*

The area of Jurong in Western Singapore stretches from West Coast Road to Tuas West Drive. It is home to Jurong Bird Park, which boasts the world's largest walk-in aviary, **The Waterfall Aviary**. Here, more than 1 000 birds from South

Chinese Garden with pagoda in background

J. Gilbert/Michelin

America and Africa fly about freely, allowing visitors to watch them feed and roost as they would in their natural habitats. The **African Wetlands** re-creates the African ecosystem (complete with African huts). Learn to feed and handle falcons during a half-hour instructional seminar. The **Lory Loft**, representing the Australian Outback, is home to species of lories from Australia, Indonesia and Papua New Guinea. Visitors view the birds in this walk-in aviary from elevated walkways and suspension bridges 12m/39ft from the ground. Other attractions here include **Pelican Pool**, **Penguin Expedition** and **World of Darkness,** where day is turned to night for nocturnal birds.

Lory at Jurong Bird Park

J. Gilbert/Michelin

## Chinese Garden★ & Japanese Garden★

*1 Chinese Garden. From the city, take the ECP and continue onto the Ayer Rajah Expressway (AYE). Take the exit towards Pan Island Expressway (PIE) and turn right at Jalan Ahmad Ibrahim. Take the exit towards Yuan Ching Road and turn right at Japanese Garden Road. Then turn right at Chinese Garden Road. Main garden open daily 6am–11pm. 6261 3632. www.jtc.gov.sg.*

The Chinese Garden is largely inspired by ancient northern China's landscaping style. The garden is especially pretty during **Mid-Autumn Festival** when adults and children roam the grounds with multicoloured lanterns and attend cultural and acrobatic performances. Reached by a bridge from the Chinese Garden, the Japanese Garden stands in stark contrast with its minimalist style.

# OUTDOOR ACTIVITIES

Many outdoor activities in Singapore are based on the sea or the nature reserves. But some activities do not rely on the natural surroundings, such as the **Reverse Bungy Experience** at **Clarke Quay★★** *(page 50)* and the many created activities on **Sentosa** island *(see FOR KIDS)*.

## ACTIVITY SPORTS

Favourite sports in Singapore are the more leisurely pursuits such as golf and bowling, but **cycling** in East Coast Park, and **off-road biking** in **Pasir Ris Park**, as well as windsurfing, sailing and water skiing, are also possible.

### Golf

Golf faciliities in Singapore are plentiful, with top quality courses open to non-members. The oldest course in Singapore, dating to 1891, was the Royal Singapore Golf Club, now the **Singapore Island Country Club**. For information: www.sicc.org.sg.

- **Jurong Country Club**
9 Science Centre Road, 6560 5655, www.jcc.org.sg.
- **Laguna Golf Club**
11 Laguna Golf Green, 6248 1777/ 8/9, www.lagunagolf.com.sg.
- **Orchid Country Club**
1 Orchid Club Road, 6750 2111, www.orchidclub.com.
- **Raffles Country Club**
450 Jalan Ahmad Ibrahim, 6861 7655, www.rcc.org.sg.

**Golf**

On all golf courses in Singapore, players must have caddies. Golf carts are advised since walking the course in 84 percent humidity is not recommended. If walking, always keep bottled water at hand.

- **Sentosa Island Golf Club**
27 Bukit Manis Road, 6275 0022, www.sentosa.com.sg.

### Cycling

The flat cycleway that skirts the sea along **East Coast Park** is the best place to ride in safety. Bikes can be rented from kiosks along the parkway. On **Sentosa** there is a rental service for biking round the island. Fees vary from S$4 to S$8 per hour; some rental companies require a S$20–S$50 deposit.

#### Road

- **Our Family Corner**
East Coast Park (mountain bikes, tandem and kids bikes).
- **Sentosa Bicycle Hire**
Kiosks for bike hire can be found at the various beaches on the island.

#### Off-Road

- **Pasir Ris Park**
Rent-a-Bike Kiosk, 51 Pasir Ris Green, Pasir Ris Car Park C. Open daily 9am–8pm. 6582 4297.

## Water Sports

The east coast and the islands, especially, offer opportunities to enjoy water sports.

### Scuba Diving

Diving possibilities are abundant in the waters to the east of Singapore, where Malaysian islands such as **Tioman** have become favourite weekend retreats for Singaporeans.

Specialist organisations can arrange local dives.

- **Big Bubble Centre** 57 Cantonment Road, 6222 6862, www.bigbubble.com.
- **Diventures Scuba** Block S, 17 Pandan Loop, 6778 0661, www.diventures.com.sg.

### Windsurfing and Sailing

For dragon boating, kayaking, powerboating, sailing and wind-surfing courses and activities, try:

- **Water Venture** 9 King George's Avenue, 6340 5335, www.water-venture.org.sg.

East Coast Park is the best place to enjoy safe windsurfing and sailing.

- **Pasta Fresca Sea Sports Centre** 1212 East Coast Parkway, 6449 1855.

### Swimming

There are some good swimming beaches on Sentosa island, namely **Siloso★★ Palawan★** and **Tanjong★** *(see map in FOR KIDS)*. Also check out:

- **Sentosa Island Resort** 800-736-8672, www.sentosa.com.sg.

## SPECTATOR SPORTS

Singapore's regular fixtures like S League football, horse racing and golf majors are spiced up by Formula1 Grand Prix night races, cricket and polo matches.

### Cricket

Home to the Singapore Cricket Club since 1852, the **Padang★★** hosts Singapore's famous cricket ground, where spectators can sprawl on the grass under a tree. One of the year's most popular events is the National Day Sixes. Check local newspapers and the SCA website. *Season: Mar–Sept.*

- **Singapore Cricket Assn.** 31 Stadium Crescent, Kallang, 6348 6566, www.cricket.org.sg.
- **Singapore Cricket Club** Connaught Drive, 6338 9271 www.scc.org.sg.

### Dragon Boat Racing

Of the five annual races, the highlight is June's **Singapore Dragon Boat Festival**, with more than 40 teams. The scenic **Singapore River Regatta** *(Nov)*, with more than 100 teams, is held in Boat Quay. Teams practise every

*Palawan Beach, Sentosa*

J. Gilbert/Michelin

weekend at Kallang Water Sports Centre, complete with drummer, although they use less ornate practice boats.

◆ **Singapore Dragon Boat Assn.**
Kallang Water Sports Centre
10 Stadium Lane, Kallang
6440 9763, www.sdba.org.sg.

## Football

Of the 12 teams, including those from Japan, China and Korea, Singapore Armed Forces Football Club and Tampines Rovers have been champions of both cup and league in recent years. Grounds are scattered within different suburbs; Jalan Besar in Lavendar is the largest. The **RHB Singapore Cup** is a huge draw. Early qualifiers for the national team, nicknamed the **Lions**, for the 2010 World Cup have been positive. *Season: Feb–Nov.*

◆ **Football Assn. of Singapore**
100 Tyrwhitt Road
#01–02 Jalan Besar Stadium
6348 3477, www.sleague.com.

## Horse Racing

Races are held regularly on Fri (evenings) and Sat and Sun (afternoons) at the high-tech racecourse in Kranji in Northern Singapore. Ticket types are matched by confusing dress codes: the Public Grandstand on Levels 1 and 2 are the cheapest, and most raucous (S$3, jeans and T-shirts allowed), progressing up to the air-conditioned Hibiscus restaurant on Level 3 (S$20, smart casual attire). The highlight of the racing year is the **Singapore International Racing Festival** held in May.

◆ **Singapore Turf Club**
1 Turf Club Avenue
Singapore Racecourse
6879 1000, www.turfclub.com.sg.

## Polo

The prestigious Singapore Polo Club, a members-only club, is open to visitors to watch tournaments and practice sessions. The annual highlight is the **Cartier International Polo Tournament**, where international teams compete with all the pomp of polo the world over. There are year-round friendly matches with visiting international teams, and practice sessions are held on Tue and Thu (evenings) and Sat and Sun (afternoons), weather permitting. Phone in advance to check.

◆ **Singapore Polo Club**
80 Mount Pleasant Road
6854 3999, www.singapore poloclub.org.

**Dragon Boat Festival**

This festival is historically the most important event of the dragon boating year. Held on the fifth day of the fifth lunar month, it honours the death of Qu Yuan during China's Chou dynasty more than 2 000 years ago. Legend has it that patriotic poet Qu, angry with government corruption, threw himself into the Mei Lo river. To save him, fishermen searched the river, thrashing their oars and beating drums to prevent his being eaten by fish. Today's dragon boat races blend this ancient tradition with a modern, exciting sporting attraction.

### Singapore F1™: Making History

Motor-racing fans flock to Singapore every September for Formula 1 Grand Prix night races. Singapore made history by hosting the island's biggest ever sporting event—F1's first ever night race in 2008. The 5km/3mi route circles the downtown Marina area, taking in Singapore's skyline plus historic landmarks like the Padang, City Hall (best seen from the Padang Grandstand) and the Singapore Flyer. Kicking off at 8pm, 1 500 mammoth lighting projectors, part of the state-of-the-art lighting system designed by world-renowned Valerio Mailo, illuminate the track to meet requirements of drivers and also High Definition TV broadcast standards. This is a huge logistical project, with over 100km/62mi of power cables and 240 steel pylons to pump out over 3 million watts. And if that sounds bright, the track is nearly four times brighter than a typical stadium.

## Motor Racing

The **Singtel Singapore Grand Prix**, held late September, is the 15th race of the **Formula 1** season. This exciting race is Singapore's biggest-ever sporting event, so demand is high for tickets, which start going on sale ten months in advance. Attendances of around 80 000 spectators include the ubiquitous corporate hospitality at premium rates, plus thousands of general grandstand passes available from mid-January. The cheapest tickets are the General Walkabout tickets starting at S$128. Go online to see the course, which is in the heart of the city, the locations of the seating, as well as the prices.

- **Formula 1™ Singtel Singapore Grand Prix**
6738 6738 (tickets);
6731 4982 (enquiries)
www.singaporegp.sg.

*Lewis Hamilton leading the Singapore Grand Prix 2009*

# FAMILY FUN

Singapore prides itself on being a place for families, and visitors will see all generations on trips out, from small children and infants to grandparents. Singapore offers plenty of activities for children of all ages, be it in the nature reserves or out on the beaches and at the theme parks. Of all the places likely to appeal to children, the most obvious would be **Sentosa** island. The theme parks, rides and beaches make it the ideal place for the whole family. Underwater World Singapore has one of the world's largest aquariums, as well as dolphin shows, which always appeal to the younger audience.

## RESORTS WORLD SENTOSA★★

*www.rwsentosa.com.*

2010 saw Sentosa live up to its lofty aims as a destination theme park with the opening of Resorts World at Sentosa. Resorts World is a new development on a massive scale. At **Universal Studios Singapore** you can ride movie rollercoasters, wrestle villains and travel to ancient times. Dive in with dolphins, or snorkel with rays at **Marine Life Park**, a huge oceanarium. At the **Maritime Xperiential Museum** you can travel back in time with pirates and the adventurers of the Maritime Silk Route. **Festive Walk** is a light, sound and water extravaganza with shopping, dining and nightlife, while the **Resorts World Casino** offers world-class gaming.

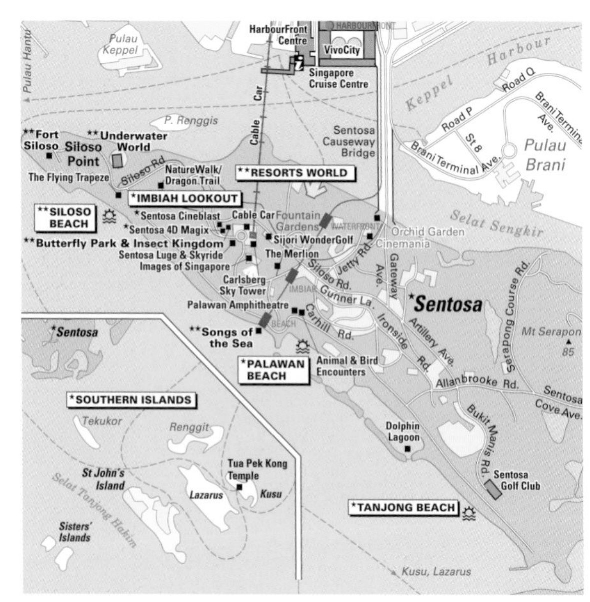

**Getting There**

**Sentosa Express** – Train *(S$3)* from VivoCity, Level 3.
**Bus** – Orange Sentosa bus *(S$3)* from HarbourFront Interchange to Beach Station. **Cable car** – From HarbourFront Station *(S$18.90 two-way, S$9.50 child, www.mountfaber.com.sg)*. **Car/taxi** – S$2 per car entry charge, plus an additional S$2 per person (applicable to passengers in taxis), as well as taxi meter charge. Motorcycles are not allowed on the island.

**Getting Around**

**Public transport** – There are five ways of getting around the island: Sentosa Express, beach trams, Fort Siloso Bus, open-top bus and Sentosa Bus. Most operate from 7am to 11pm. Car parks are readily available.

**Tickets**

The attractions on Sentosa are all independent, but admission to the island will normally cost you S$3, which includes a return trip on the Sentosa Express. Multi-attraction passes are on sale from Sentosa ticket booths.

## SENTOSA ISLAND★

Sentosa's older attractions still offer plenty of fun for big kids, plus some new surprises. *Mosquito repellent is a must for night walks.*

### Imbiah Lookout★

The cluster of attractions and cable car station at Imbiah Lookout make an excellent starting point if you have limited time on Sentosa. There are also numerous food and drink outlets and places to snap up kitschy Merlion-themed souvenirs or miniature cable car replicas. *Access via the cable car from HarbourFront, on the Blue and Red Line buses, or Sentosa Express (alight at Imbiah Station: see box).*

#### Nature Walk and Dragon Trail

Spot squirrels, macaques and more than 20 species of birds along this 1.5km/1mi route through the rain forest, which begins at the Cable Car Arrival Plaza. The Dragon Trail features rocks that are meant to resemble dragon bones.

#### Butterfly Park & Insect Kingdom★★

*Open daily 9am–6.30pm. S$16, S$10 children.*

Children can get up close and personal with some 1 500 live butterflies among the foliage of the **conservatory★★**. If you're brave, venture into the 70m/230ft-long cave lit up by fireflies, and hiding rhino beetles and scorpions. Don't miss the hands-on experience during stage shows where audience members learn how to handle giant scorpions and other insects. At the Stick Insect Safari you can touch them – if you can see them!

#### Tiger Sky Tower

*Open daily 9am–9pm. S$12, S$8 children. 6259 9288. www.skytower.com.sg.*

Spot your next destination from the top of this 110m/361ft tower said to be Asia's tallest free-standing observation tower. You can see the mainland and Southern Islands

from here, and on a clear day, Malaysia and Indonesia.

### Images of Singapore

*Open daily 9am–7pm. S$10, S$7 children.*

Catch Chinese Opera singers staging an impromptu opera, and Hindu devotees walking on hot coals during **Thaipusam**. Using uncannily lifelike figures, animatronics, special effects and rare artefacts, the museum re-creates life in Singapore from the 14C to today. This attraction is a fun and fast way for kids to absorb Singapore's history in bites, Disney-style. The explanation of the major festivals and rituals of Singapore's main ethnic groups is interesting.

### Merlion and Merlion Walk

*Open daily 10am–8pm. S$8, S$5 children.*

The legend of this half-fish, half-lion creature has grown ever since the Singapore Tourism Board thought it up in 1964; this particular iteration of the familiar beast is certainly the most gaudy (it is bathed in purple light at night, pierced by twinkling fairy lights) and features an elaborate exploration of the legend of Singapore's foundation. Sea dragons, mermaids and even Mercubs adorn the Merlion sculpture. The mosaic water fountains of the Merlion Walkway in front are said to be inspired by Gaudí.

### Sentosa 4D Magix★

*Open daily 10am–9pm. S$18, S$11 children (if 12 years and below, with a minimum height of 90cm). 6274 5355. www.sentosa4dmagix.com.sg.*

This small, nondescript film theatre is equipped with special pneumatic seats that features compressed air jets—all of which adds up to a great experience for younger kids. During the movie *Pirates*, the audience has to "shake off crabs", "dodge bullets" and get wet. Costing about S$10 000, each seat is individually controlled, so you can choose to skip the effects.

### Sentosa Cineblast★

*Open daily 10am–9pm. S$18, S$11 children (if 12 years and below, with a minimum height of 90cm). 6274 5355. www.cineblast.com.sg.*

While Sentosa 4D Magix concentrates on environmental effects, Sentosa Cineblast is about motion simulation. High-definition wide-screen projection screens and six-axis moving carts convey the sense of a swift current or sitting in the back of a race car, to accompanying 3D visuals.

## Siloso Beach★★

Located just west of Imbiah Lookout, on the southern coast of the island, this beach revs up kids' adrenaline as they race with the Sentosa Luge & Skyride.

### Underwater World Singapore★★

*80 Siloso Road. Underwater World open daily 9am–9pm. S$22.90, S$14.60 children (includes admission to Dolphin Lagoon). 6275 0030. www.underwaterworld.com.sg.*

Admire some 2 500 marine creatures at this aquarium, which features an 83m/272ft travelator and glass tunnel through a pool of stingrays, eels and turtles. There are touch pools for those who really want to get close to starfish and baby sharks. Real marine-life fans can dive with the animals, and pick their ideal companions: sharks, dolphins or dugong.

### Sentosa Luge & Skyride

*Open daily 10am–9.30pm. S$11 Luge & Skyride combo.*

This is a sedate but nonetheless enjoyable ride down a gently curving slope in a small cart. Visitors take the Skyride (a simple chairlift) up to the start of the course for a bird's-eye look at the island. The course ends at Siloso Beach.

### Songs of the Sea★★

*Beach Station. Shows daily at 7.40pm, 8.40pm. S$10.*

This multimedia extravaganza revolves around the suspiciously familiar tale of how a young man meets a sleeping princess who is under a spell. Designed by Yves Pepin, responsible for similar productions at Disneyland Tokyo, the show combines enough pyrotechnics and computer imaging to make the story feel brand new.

## Palawan Beach★

Sitting just east of Imbiah Lookout, on the southern coast of Sentosa, this beach offers kids an opportunity to get up close and personal with pythons, monkeys and dolphins.

### Animal and Bird Encounters

*Palawan Amphitheatre.*

Children will have to be dragged away from the fun-filled animal shows here, which feature parrots, pig-tailed macaques, Siberian Huskies and other animals. Don't be afraid to cuddle up with the Burmese Albino Rock Python for a little companionship.

### Dolphin Lagoon

*Palawan Beach. Open daily 10.30am–6pm. Dolphin shows at 11am*, 1pm, 3.30pm, 5.30pm daily (*training session on weekdays, usual show on weekends and public holidays). S$22.90, S$14.60 children*

Singapore Zoological Gardens

Singapore Tourism Board

*(includes admission to Underwater World). 6275 0030. www.underwaterworld.com.sg.*

If you have visited Underwater World Singapore, it is worth seeing Dolphin Lagoon to complete the experience. If just meeting the adorable pink dolphins (Indo-Pacific Humpback Dolphins) isn't enough, visitors can swim with them for a more personal encounter. The "Swim with the Dolphins" package (*S$150*) includes a ride around the lagoon as well as instruction on the hand cues used to interact and communicate with the dolphins.

## SINGAPORE ZOO★★★

*80 Mandai Lake Road. Open daily 8.30am–6pm. S$18, S$9 children. Tram ride tours S$5, S$2.50 children. 6269 3411. www.zoo.com.sg.*

Located next to Night Safari ***(see page 85)***, this "open concept" zoo is one of the most popular attractions in Singapore. It sits in the north of the island, in Mandai, off the Tampines Expressway, and attracts one and a half million visitors a year. A highlight of the zoo experience for both kids and adults is the **Jungle Breakfast with Wildlife** at 9am with orang-utans and petite cotton top tamarins.

Spread over 28ha/69 acres, with monkeys and peacocks scurrying around freely, the zoo tries to simulate **natural environments** for its inhabitants by using discreet dry or wet moats rather than bars or screens for containment. Forty of the species displayed are on the world's endangered list, and the zoo is particularly proud of its large colony of **Bornean orang-utans**. In all 33 have been bred in captivity.

Another favourite is the first polar bear to be born in the tropics. The zoo is also home to the **white Bengal tiger**, a rarity given that only one in 1 000 tigers has this colouration. The elephant enclosure is built alongside the tranquil waters of the Seletar Reservoir. Here kids can watch Asian elephants being bathed and scrubbed by their mahouts. The **Australian Outback** zone features a few female grey kangaroos, and a number of wallabies and emus.

## EAST COAST PARK★★

*East Coast Park lies east of the city centre, along the coast. To get there, see box opposite.*

**Getting To East Coast Park**

Bus 401 to East Coast Park Service Road runs on Sunday and public holidays only. The best services to get are 16, 155 and 196 which go to Marine Crescent and Marine Terrace; walk across using the underpasses or overhead bridge. Service 36 stops outside Marine Parade shopping centre and is available from the city. An hourly shuttle bus service operates between Parkway Parade and Playground @ Splash. By car, take East Coast Parkway; exit at Still Road. Turn right at Marine Parade Road, then right at Telok Kurau Road to continue on Marine Crescent. Turn left into Marine Terrace.

Downtown East/NTUC Club

Wild Wild Wet

The largest and most popular park in Singapore, East Coast Park hosts activities ranging from indoor mini golf to Tai Chi. A new 42km/26mi long **Eastern Coastal Park Connector Network** links the park to other parks in Eastern Singapore such as Pasir Ris Park.

## Playground @ Big Splash

*902 East Coast Parkway. 6345 6762. www.playground.com.sg.*

This venue tore down its famous water slides to make way for sporting and playing facilities, as well as mid-scale fast-food cafés and restaurants that appeal to adults and children. One of the attractions is the indoor mini-golf course **Lilliputt**.

## PASIR RIS

*From city area, head for East Coast Parkway then turn onto Tampines Expressway. Take the exit towards Loyang Avenue and turn left into Pasir Ris Drive 3. Turn right at Pasir Ris Close to reach Downtown East.*

The area of Pasir Ris, just west of Changi Airport, is a haven for children, attracted to the theme parks here.

## Wild Wild Wet

*Open Mon, Wed–Fri 1pm–7pm; Sat–Sun, public holidays 10am–7pm. S$15.50, S$10.50 children. 6581 9128. www.wildwildwet.com.*

This water theme park has exciting rides such as **Ular-lah**, a giant raft slide; **Tsunami**, a fun wave pool; and **Waterworks**, a series of high-speed flumes. Although most of the water rides are for older children and adults, there are plenty of safe areas for toddlers.

## Escape Theme Park

*Open Sat–Sun, school holidays, public holidays 10am–8pm. S$17.70, S$8.90 children. 6581 9112. www.escapethemepark.com.sg.*

With such heart-stopping rides as a five-and-a-half storey log boat, a **Roller Coaster** and **Go-Kart** track, this park allows families to get terrified together.

# PERFORMING ARTS

Every night out in Singapore can be special, given the variety of entertainment available. The difficulty is choosing among all the artistic and cultural performances on offer. After visiting a nightclub one night, you can attend the Chinese Opera or the theatre, a ballet performance or a concert on subsequent evenings.

## Classical Music and Opera

### Singapore Symphony Orchestra

*11 Empress Place, Victoria Concert Hall. 6338 1230. www.sso.org.sg.*

The much respected Singapore Symphony Orchestra was formed in 1980 and successfully managed to bridge the gap between music of the East and West, performing every weekend at Esplanade - Theatres on the Bay. While the majority of its concerts specialise in Western classical composers, there is also a strong commitment to promoting new Asian composers and compositions.

Chinese Theatre Circle

Chinese Theatre Circle

### Singapore Lyric Opera

*Stamford Arts Centre, #03–06 155 Waterloo Street. 6336 1929. www.singaporeopera.com.sg.*

The Singapore Lyric Opera was officially formed in 1990, and has produced works as diverse as a contemporary staging of Rossini's *The Barber of Seville* and an opera written by local composer Leong Yon Pin. Most of the performances are at the Esplanade and Victoria Concert Hall *(see below)*.

### Singapore Symphony Chorus

*11 Empress Place, Victoria Concert Hall. 6338 1230. www.symphony chorus.sg.*

Singapore Symphony Chorus was created in 1981, selecting from local church and university choirs, which enabled the SSO to expand its repertoire. Recent performances include Handel's *Messiah* and Beethoven's *Choral Symphony*, with popular classics in between.

### Victoria Concert Hall

*11 Empress Place. MRT: City Hall or Raffles Place. 6338 4401. www.vch.org.sg.*

This venue is Singapore's most historic concert hall *(see COLONIAL DISTRICT)*.

**Chinese Opera – the Drama**

More like a performance of a folk tale on stage, Chinese Opera has dwindled in popularity over the past few years. An art form in itself, Beijing Opera has been performed in Singapore for more than 100 years; it was once the most popular form of entertainment, especially during Chinese festivals. Spurred by the decline, attempts are being made to revive it. In 2005 world history was made when the Chinese Theatre Circle performed '*Intrigues in the Qing Imperial Court*' in English, part of the Chinese Cultural Festival, using a multiracial cast. Although performances of full-length operas (which may last more than three hours) are held at conventional theatres, the Chinese Theatre Circle aims to make the genre more approachable, especially for foreign visitors.

## Chinese Music & Opera

### Singapore Chinese Orchestra

*Singapore Conference Hall, 7 Shenton Way. 6440 3839. www.sco.com.sg.*

Regular performances by the Singapore Chinese Orchestra include fortnightly concerts at the Singapore Conference Hall, several concerts a year at the Esplanade, plus participation in many of Singapore's leading music events. The orchestra reaches a wider audience with outdoor concerts in national parks, and encourages new commissions from Southeast Asian composers. Concerts are often a medley of popular opera, and musical and folk tunes, using traditional Chinese instruments.

### Chinese Theatre Circle

*5 Smith Street. MRT: Chinatown. 6323 4862. www.ctcopera.com.sg.*

Instead of an orthodox theatre performance of Chinese opera, which can last more than three hours, recitals given by the Chinese Theatre Circle offer visitors a palatable introduction to the art. Performed in the unorthodox surroundings of the **Chinese Opera Teahouse**, a renovated shophouse, the recitals are an easier way than a full-blown opera to come to grips with the art. An evening entitled "Sights and Sounds of Chinese Opera" *(Fri–Sat 7pm–9pm; S$35)* begins with a meal, followed by a talk and a demonstration of the art, ending with a colourful performance of opera excerpts *(English subtitles)*.

## Theatre

Theatrical productions in Singapore waver between those of touring companies from London's West End and Singaporean takes on classic plays. Drama has become more creative in the last decade, but the state censor's pen is always at the ready to check scripts before they take to the stage.

### Esplanade - Theatres on the Bay

*1 Esplanade Drive, Marina. MRT: City Hall then 10-minute walk. 6828 8377. www.esplanade.com.*

This heavyweight venue covers a mammoth six acres, and is the

theatre of choice for overseas touring companies. It offers a plethora of festivals year-round and performances by home-grown groups. its facilities include the 2 000-seat theatre and 1 600-seat concert hall, both with world-class acoustics, plus recital studios and outdoor spaces for free concerts.

### Singapore Repertory Theatre

*DBS Arts Centre, 20 Merbau Road. MRT: Clarke Quay then taxi. 6221 5585. www.srt.com.sg*

With its home at the DBS Arts Centre, this repertory company aims to produce English-language theatre while promoting the "Asian spirit" and occasionally hosting illuminati such as the Royal Shakespeare Company.

**Cutting-Edge Drama**

Local theatre has seen the introduction of cutting-edge subject matter in recent years. One of the most courageous groups is W!ld Rice, which uses local talent and where possible, new Singaporean writers. It aims to push the boundaries, and in 2007 staged *Happy Endings – Asian Boys Vol 3*, a gay trilogy, at the same time the gay issue (homosexuality is illegal in Singapore) was being discussed in Parliament. Seven years earlier, The Necessary Stage performed *Asian Boys Vol 1*, which raised eyebrows. Its production of *Good People*, which marked its 20th anniversary, tackled topics of drugs, death and the death penalty.

### Jubilee Hall

*Level 3, Raffles Hotel Arcade, 1 Beach Road. MRT: City Hall. 6337 1886.*

In addition to Singapore's major theatrical venues, Jubilee Hall in the Raffles Hotel is a recently renovated Victorian-style theatre playhouse with varied repertoires.

### The Arts House

*1 Old Parliament Lane. MRT: Clarke Quay then taxi. 6332 6900. www.theartshouse.com.sg.*

This venue is Singapore's newest multi-disciplinary arts centre, open since 2004. It is housed in an 1827 building, previously the Court House and Parliament House.

### The Substation

*45 Armenian Street. Box Office open Mon–Fri 12pm–8.30pm, Sat–Sun two hours before performance. 6337 7535. www.substation.org.*

Founded in 1990 on the grounds of an electrical substation, this was the city's first independent contemporary arts centre. It showcases traditional dance, local rock bands, experimental theatre, poetry readings, international art exhibits and film festivals. It's a good place to test the vibrancy of Singapore's "alternative" culture.

### Victoria Theatre

*9 Empress Place. MRT: City Hall or Raffles Place. 6338 8283. www.nac.gov.sg.*

This British Neoclassical landmark in the Colonial District was Singapore's principal theatre from 1905. It is now playing second fiddle to the Esplanade.

*The Importance of Being Earnest by W!ld Rice*

W!ld Rice

### W!ld Rice

*3A Kerbau Road. MRT: Little India. 6292 2695. www.wildrice.com.sg.*

Cutting-edge drama from W!ld Rice uses the notoriety of highly-respected Artistic Director Ivan Heng, with new and original works from local writers ***(see box opposite)***. New interpretations of world classics include their recent pantomime ***Jack & the Beansprout!*** and ***Blithe Spirit***, adapted and set in a Singapore housing estate.

## Dance

### Bhaskar's Arts Academy

*Stamford Arts Centre, 155 Waterloo Street. MRT: Little India. 6336 6537. www.bhaskarsartsacademy.com*

This academy is devoted to Indian dance. Its Nrityalaya Aesthetics Society comprises professional ***kathakali*** dancers and musicians who teach the unique art from Kerala, south India. Known for its colourful make-up and costumes, ***kathakali*** uses intricate eye movement and hand gestures to tell the story. Performances also include traditional Tamil, and the solo performance ***bharatya natyam***.

### ECNAD

*#04–07 Telok Ayer Performing Arts Centre, 182 Cecil Street. MRT: Tanjong Pagar. 6226 6404 or 6226 6772 . www.ecnad.org.*

This contemporary dance troupe (dance spelt backwards) uses surreal choreography, sets and costumes to accompany its movement and sound. In addition to The Arts House, Victoria Theatre and the Esplanade, performances have also been held at fountains, building atriums and night spots.

*ECNAD performing at the Mercedes-Benz Asia Fashion Award 2006*

Melinda Ng/ECNAD

### Singapore Dance Theatre

*Level 2, Fort Canning Centre, Cox Terrace. MRT: Dhoby Ghaut. 6338 0611. www.singaporedance theatre.com.*

Representing classical dance, this theatre excels in ballet. Its annual highlight is Ballet Under the Stars in Fort Canning Park, in July. Other performances are held at the Esplanade. Recent stagings include ***Giselle, Coppelia*** and ***Swan Lake***.

# SHOPPING

A national obsession, shopping is one of Singapore's magnetic charms. Mega-malls offer top international brands, while Orchard Road, Chinatown and Little India have their own character. Bartering is quite acceptable in the markets and at some smaller retailers. Singaporeans love to barter and rarely pay the full price for anything, so join in and see what bargains you can find.

## Before You Buy

**Opening Hours** – Most mall shop hours are 10am–9pm, sometimes earlier on Sundays and until 10pm on Saturdays. Some malls are open until 11pm on Saturdays (Paragon, Wisma Atria, Centrepoint, Tangs Orchard). Independent shops open later on Sundays, or not at all. In Chinatown and Little India, markets come to life at night and close about 10pm. Haji Lane boutique stores open around 2pm.

**Public Conveniences** – Shopping malls and department stores have clean, well-maintained facilities.

**GST and Tax Refund** – The Goods and Services Tax of 7 percent is chargeable on all goods. Tourists can get a GST refund (*www.globalrefund.com; 6225 6238*) on goods over S$100 when flying out of Singapore within two months of purchase. Some stores (including Mustafa Centre and Sim Lim Square) offer the refund on the spot, for which your passport and return air ticket are required. When purchasing at stores with the Tax Free or Global Refund logo, request the GST refund form, which should be stamped when you present your passport. Receipts, forms and goods must be produced at the airport before boarding to claim your refund. A small service charge will be deducted from the amount.

**Guarantees & Warranties** – Most electrical and computer items come with a one-year warranty, which may not be valid back home. Check with the retailer, or do research in advance. If you're shopping for jewellery, especially gold, jade and gems, look out for the QJS sticker (*Quality Jewellers of Singapore; 6458 6377; www.qjs.org.sg*) for reassurance that it's the real deal.

*VivoCity, HarbourFront*

VivoCity

## Chinatown and CBD

A combination of tourist-friendly streets and gentrified shophouses, Chinatown is a most entertaining shopping area. Chic boutiques have sprung up around Ann Siang and Erskine roads.

**Asylum** *(22 Ann Siang Road, MRT: Chinatown/Tanjong Pagar, Mon–Fri noon–9pm, Sat noon–7pm, 6324*

MUST DO

Chinatown vendors

J. Gilbert/Michelin

*2289, www.theasylum.com.sg)* is part gallery, part design company with a quirky collection of local designers' latest urban wear, Surface To Air T-shirts, Cargo bags and CDs of local bands on its new music label Asylum Sounds.

**Books Actually** *(5 Ann Siang Road, MRT: Chinatown/Tanjong Pagar, Mon–Sat 11am–9pm, 6221 1170, www.booksactually.com*) is the new home for literature specialists, mainly English with some antique editions. Occasional poetry readings, plus their own hand-stitched notebooks, are offered.

**Cayen** *(2/F, 54A Club Street, MRT: Chinatown/Tanjong Pagar, Mon–Fri noon–8pm, Sat 11am–6pm, 6227 6187, www.cayen.com.sg)* sells custom-made clothes for women, with fittings available. Top-quality cotton casuals, formal evening-wear and ready-to-wear.

**Chinatown Night Market** *(Trengganu and Pagoda streets, MRT: Chinatown, Sun–Thu 5pm–11pm, Fri–Sat 5pm–1am, 6372 0478*) is the place to stock up on (cheap) clothes and souvenirs. Street stalls sell everything from chopstick sets, to paper dragons, appliquéd bags and Chinese goodies. Prices are "fixed", but good-natured haggling is expected.

At **Da Wei Arts & Crafts** *(270 South Bridge Road, MRT: Chinatown, daily 11am–7pm, 6224 5058),* ignore the paintings on the wall, and head for good-value calligraphy brushes to experiment with back home,

**Great Singapore Sale**

If you thought Singapore was already shopping mad, watch it go up a couple of gears during the two-month high-octane shopping frenzy encompassing the whole city. The main hub is Orchard Road, where discounts of up to 70 percent are proffered to tempt even the most fervent non-consumerist, with even larger discounts to tourists (bring your passport to get the discount card). During the sale, usually held from late May to late July, shopping hours are extended and a festive atmosphere ensues city-wide. Get a copy of the brochure upon your arrival to discover the best deals. Then wear comfortable shoes and get shopping!

ranging in size from a couple of hairs to floor-mop thickness.

**Eu Yan Sang** *(269 South Bridge Road, MRT: Chinatown, Mon–Sat 8.30am–6pm, other branches city wide, 6223 6333, www.euyansang.com),* going strong since 1879, is a traditional Chinese medicine hall that sells lotions and potions ranging from bird's nest with wild American ginseng to Lingzhi cracked spores. The adjacent clinic offers English consultations.

**Hayden** *(88 Club Street, MRT: Chinatown, Tue–Sat noon–7pm, Sun noon–6pm, 6220 0882),* a local designer, has bold sequinned gowns and retro Victoriana with white lacy tops and silk collarless coats, all from top European fabrics. Look out for Michel Negrin accessories.

**Li-Hong Jade** *(20 Smith Street, MRT: Chinatown, Tue–Sun 10.30am–7.30pm, 6323 3919, www.lihongjade.com)* has an outstanding choice of top jade, plus advice on different qualities and colours, as well as coral. Staff can custom-make a setting using braiding to transform your piece into a necklace or bracelet.

**Ming Fang Antique House** *(274 South Bridge Road, MRT: Chinatown, daily 11am–7pm, 6224 3788)* is heaving with jade pendants, Buddha heads, brass dragons and a kitschy collection of Mao statues. English is spoken enough to haggle.

**Singapore Handicraft Centre** *(Chinatown Point, 133 New Bridge Road, MRT: Chinatown, usually 11am–8pm)* has four floors of handicraft shops, from **jade carvings** to calligraphy, bronze statues and traditional Chinese musical instruments.

**Style: Nordic** *(39 Ann Siang Road, MRT: Chinatown, Mon–Sat noon–8pm, Sun noon–5pm, 6423 9114, www.stylenordic.com)* has a huge lifestyle showroom with Scandinavian-only brands and designers, including **urban fashion** labels Nudie Jeans, Filippa K and Pour Femme. Simple Finnish glassware, Artek's iconic furniture and other homewear are on hand.

**Time of Tea** *(38 Mosque Street, MRT: Chinatown, daily 10am–7pm, 6220 5620)* sells top Chinese teas as well as tiny ceramic tea sets. Its knowledgeable staff will give you a crash course in tea, including how to choose, make and drink it.

**View Point** *(China Square Central, 18 Cross Street #02–09, MRT: Chinatown, Mon–Fri 11am–7.30pm, Sat–Sun 9am–7pm, 6536 5320, www.viewpointtrading.com),* crammed with antiques and collectables, is the highlight of the weekend market in the same building. You'll find old HMV gramophones, 1960s Cantonese wedding dresses, Chinese *wayang* (opera) vinyl, 1950s advertising posters and more.

**Yue Hwa Chinese Products Store** *(70 Eu Tong Sen Street, MRT: Chinatown, Sun–Fri 11am–9pm, Sat 11am–10pm, 6538 9233, www.yuehwa.com.sg),* a Chinatown landmark, was built as a hotel in 1927; it now houses a classic collection of Chinese products with speciality teas, silk scarves and traditional Chinese clothing. One floor is devoted to dried foods and cooking.

## Colonial District

**Raffles Hotel Arcade** is a must for the boutiques that ooze style surrounding the graceful courtyard. Elsewhere, **Suntec City**

**Mall** is Singapore's second-biggest mall, with some 100 F&B outlets alone.

**Artfolio** *(328 North Bridge Road, #02–25 Raffles Hotel Arcade, MRT: City Hall, Mon–Sat 11am–7pm, Sun 12pm–5pm, 6334 4677, www.artfolio.com.sg)* is a small commercial gallery with regular exhibits of paintings and sculptures by southeast Asian artists, mainly working in bold oils.

**Funan DigitaLife Mall** *(109 North Bridge Road, MRT: City Hall, daily 10.30am–8.30pm, 6336 8327, www.funan.com.sg)* boasts six well-organised levels of reputable IT stores, with most of the eletronics and computers between levels 3 and 6. The top floor has a great **food court**, perfect to refuel after a splurge on gadgets.

Classy boutique **Golden Silk** *(328 North Bridge Road, #02–11 Raffles Hotel Arcade, MRT: City Hall, Mon–Sat 10am–8pm, Sun 10am–3pm, 6333 1930, www.golden-silk.com)* offers a shimmering selection of brightly coloured  **silks,** women's separates and formal eveningwear, all from Singaporean designers. Alterations are free.

**Harris Books** *(#02–69/71 Suntec City Mall, MRT: City Hall, daily 10.30am–9.30pm, also branch at airport, 6514 6699, www.harrisbook.com)* is a decent chain with a mainstream selection.

At **Laichan** *(328 North Bridge Road, #02–10 Raffles Hotel Arcade, MRT: City Hall, daily 11am–8pm, 6338 4806)* fashion designer Laichan shows off feminine chic and dramatic formal eveningwear, including edgy one-off *cheongsams* with semi-precious stones. Artwork by his brother Eddie is also for sale.

*Silk shirt from Golden Silk*

Golden Silk

**MPH Raffles City** *(B1–24/26 Raffles City, 252 North Bridge Road, MRT: City Hall, daily 10am–10pm, 6336 4232, www.mph.com.sg)* has a huge selection of popular fiction and get-rich-quick paperbacks, plus books and maps on Singapore and regional cuisine.

**Tembusu Art Gallery** *(#01-05 MICA Building, 140 Hill Street, MRT: City Hall, Tue–Sun 1pm–9pm, 6337 1027, www.tembusu-art.com.sg)*, established in 2006, specialises in emerging southeast Asian artists. Exhibits change every month; all items are for sale.

## Little India

Of all Singapore's historic shopping areas, Little India has probably retained its original charm best of all, its white painted

### Local Colour

Sundays are chaotically crowded in Little India, with most immigrant workers from the Indian subcontinent coming here for socialising and shopping. For a glimpse into the past, take a peek into the fragrant 174 Serangoon Road, where locals bring their bags of spices to get them ground in industrial-sized grinders.

**Singapore Markets**

Although there are a lot of "wet markets" in the suburban areas, where locals buy meat, fish, fruit and vegetables from a no-frills covered market, there is a surprising lack of street markets for clothes, antiques and the like. The few exceptions are a welcome addition. Sungei Road, also dubbed **Thieves Market**, sprawls out over several streets near Little India where dealers (or just locals getting rid of junk) spread the items on the pavement; haggling is essential. Once known as the Flea Market at Clarke Quay, the stalls have now shifted to the weekend market at **China Square Central**, with two floors of stalls selling antiques and collectables. Chinatown's Pagoda and Trengganu streets have tourist-friendly street markets, perfect for hunting souvenirs and Chinese satin clothes.

shophouses still selling jasmine, vegetables, Bollywood DVDs, gold and saucepans, handicrafts and bangles, with wonderful pit-stops for food. Gold hunters head to the jewellery shops clustered around **Serangoon Road**, while **Campbell Lane** has the aroma of jasmine garlands at the flower stalls.

**Celebration of Arts** *(2 Dalhousie Lane, MRT: Little India, daily 9am–10pm, 6392 0769)* holds an attractive mix of Indian handicrafts, from bronze Buddhas to carved wood screens, Hindu gods in brass and silk shawls.

At **Chandhini Jewellery** *(97 Serangoon Road, MRT: Little India, Mon–Sat 10.30am–8pm, 6299 0595, www.chandhinijewellery.com),* gems and semi-precious stones, based on original designs influenced by Bollywood movies and antique Rajasthan style, are elaborately set in gold (oxidised to suit European tastes) or silver. The results are tasteful rather than flashy.

**Jamal Kazura Aromatics** *(131 Dunlop Street, MRT: Little India, Mon–Sat 9.30am–6pm, 6392 1978),* a tiny fragrance boutique, blends natural oils for perfume, burning or massage, based on the traditional craft of ***attars*** (Arabic perfume oils). They are sold in small glass vials. Choose your own blend of custom-made scent *(main branch: 21 Bussorah Street).*

At **Little India Arcade** *(Hasting Road and Campbell Lane, MRT: Little India, daily approx 9am–10pm),* shophouses on the outside sell flowers, fruit and Bollywood garb, Indian handicrafts and silks to a soundtrack of Hindi music. Inside, stalls offer jewelled boxes, glittery bangles and henna tattoos.

**Mustafa Centre** *(145 Syed Alwi Road, MRT: Farrer Park, daily 24hr daily, 6295 5855, www.mustafa.com.sg)* draws crowds for fixed-price electronics, luggage and computers. What this vast department store lacks in charm it makes up for in no-nonsense value. Avoid busy Sundays.

**Sungei Road Fleamarket** *(Sungei Road, Pasar Lane and Larut Road, MRT: Bugis, daily approx 10am–7pm)* is a genuine street market with a collection of junk and gems, from wooden trunks to dusty porcelain to vinyl records. Vague hours; busiest at weekends from 1pm on.

**Tekka Centre** *(corner of Buffalo and Serangoon roads, closed for redevel-*

*opment; moved to temporary plot on Race Course Road, MRT: Little India),* a no-frills wet market housed in a concrete building, has meat, fish, fruit and vegetable stalls on Level 1, with cheap and cheerful **Indian clothing** on Level 2.

## Arab Quarter and Bugis

Once the hub of the **textile** trade, the area around **Arab Street** has enjoyed a revival in recent years. Clustered around **Haji Lane** near Sultan Mosque, once rundown shops have reopened as quirky boutiques with fresh fashions. Style and content seem a world away from the more conventional textile shops on Arab Street, and even their business hours are different, often not opening their doors till around 1pm, closing at 8pm. **Bugis**, one-time haunt of sailors and prostitutes, has smartened up—slightly. Indoor markets hold cheap, cheerful stalls.

**Alta Moda** *(92 Arab Street, MRT: Bugis, Mon–Sat 9.30am–6.30pm, Sun 11am–5.30pm, 6296 7117)* has a superb collection of fabrics that includes Korean tule embroidery; it is the sole distributor of Carvalli, Valentino and Armani fabric designs. Prices per meter range from S$9 to S$3 000 (heavily beaded Chantilly lace with Swarovski crystal). Suits take around three days to make.

At **Basharahil House of Batik** *(101 Arab Street, MRT: Bugis, Mon–Sat 10am–6pm, Sun 11am–5pm, 6293 6569)* find colourful and affordable swathes of **Indonesian batik,** including men's and women's shirts, bags, and fabric by the meter.

**Bugis Village** *(Rochor Road, MRT: Bugis, daily, most stalls noon–10pm)* has a cheap and colourful collection of bags, clothes and copy watches in rows of tightly packed stalls. It's hugely popular with locals and crowded every evening.

**Designed in Singapore** *(24 Mohamed Sulktan Road, MRT: Bugi, daily 1pm–8pm, 6733 9954, www.designedinsingapore.com)* succeeds with a collaboration of young Singaporean design graduates and a huge showroom showcasing innovative furniture, laptop bags and fashion.

At **Dulcetfig** *(41 Haji Lane, MRT: Bugis, Mon–Fri 2pm–10pm, Sat–Sun 2pm–11pm, 6396 5648),* owner Lovie Wong designed most of the clothes, an eccentric collection of **urban wear,** plus retro gear including Anonymous Apparel T-shirts. Accessories include some chunky jewellery and sequinned "baguette" bags by Lulu.

**Old School Style**

In 2007 the renovated Methodist Girls School on Mount Sophia became Old School (*11 Mount Sophia; www.oldschool.sg*), its six blocks transformed into a hip artists' area. With a cinema, outdoor café, fashion stores and bistros, it aims to become a centre for local artists and musicians. For shoppers here, highlights include **2902 Gallery** (*11B #B2-09; www.2902gallery.com*), which exhibits and sells contemporary photography. **CitySpace** has unusual hand-made furniture by a Filipino design collective. Watch out for more studios and stores in the future.

**The Heritage Shop** *(#01–01, 93 Jalan Sultan, MRT: Bugis/Lavender, daily 1pm–8pm, 6223 7982),* Patrick Phoa's domain, has thousands of collectibles, from Peranakan tiffin tins to old advertising signs that often make it to the stage as props in local theatre productions.

**Know It Nothing** *(51 Haji Lane, MRT: Bugis, Mon–Sat 1pm–8pm, Sun 3pm–7pm, 6392 5475, www.knowitnothing.com)* houses a funky collection of urban menswear in a stunning modern conversion of a traditional shop, complete with sloping glass roof. Look for Julian Red jeans and Pointer Footwear.

**Royal Fabrics** *(59, 65 & 94 Arab Street, MRT: Bugis, Mon–Sat 12pm–8pm, Sun 12pm–5pm, 6396 3820, www.royalfabrics.com)* specialises in fabrics for evening gowns, including beaded chiffon, Italian lace and designs inspired by leading European fashion designers.

**Pluck** *(31–33 Haji Lane, MRT: Bugis, Mon–Sat 12pm–8pm, 6396 4048, www.pluck.com.sg)* is a tiny "style emporium" with **vintage jewellery,** cushions made from vintage scarfs and 1950s wallpaper. Have a tiramisu sundae at its adjacent ice-cream parlour.

**Salad** *(25–27 Haji Lane, MRT: Bugis, Mon–Sat 12pm–8pm, 6299 5805)* sports a simple, stark style within a predominantly black-and-white interior stocked with custom-made accessories, beaded curtains, shiny black photo frames and jute trays.

**Straits Records** *(22 Bali Lane, MRT: Bugis, daily 3pm–late, 9385 3211)* features reggae, indie and hard rock CDs and vinyl. Straits is also a record label, specialising in local punk and indie bands and organising gigs in alternative venues.

**Sim Lim Square** *(1 Rochor Canal Road, MRT: Bugis, most stores daily 10.30am–9pm, 6338 3859, www.simlimsquare.com.sg)* has six levels of electronics, computers and cameras, with every gizmo and gadget imaginable. Start at Level 6 and work your way down. For major items, shop around and check everything—go with an idea of what you want. Always ask for their "best price", especially when paying in cash or buying more than one item. GST refund available on Level 1 *(11am–7.30pm)* upon presentation of passport and air ticket.

*Fabrics in textile shop on Arab Street*

J. Gilbert/Michelin

## Orchard Road

*See map in DISTRICTS.*

Shopping is the lifeblood of the Orchard Road Area. The hub of **"mall city"**, Orchard Road is ideal for those who love traversing air-conditioned shopping centres with well-known fashion labels. Orchard malls have everything from top designers of the Chanel and Gucci variety to quirky boutiques and contemporary Indian furniture. New to Orchard Road are megamalls Orchard Central *(www.orchardcentral.com.sg)*, 313@Somerset *(www.313somerset.com.sg)* and ION Orchard *(www.ionorchard.com)*.

**Paragon** *(290 Orchard Road, daily 10am–9.30pm, 6738 5535, www.paragonsc.com.sg)* showcases a suave and relatively calm six-floor collection of designer names housed within an elegant white exterior. Brands include **Yves Saint Laurent Rive Gauche, Prada** and **Gucci**, but don't miss urban fashion from **Miss Sixty** and **Projectshop**. **Blue Canopy** has luxury but unusual household items, and Level 5 specialises in kids' clothes and toys. The basement **Food Cellar** has a deluxe supermarket, or enjoy top coffee and cakes at the **PS Cafe**.

**TANGS Orchard** *(310 and 320 Orchard Road, Mon–Thu & Sat 10.30am–9.30pm, Fri 10.30am–11pm, Sun 11am–8.30pm, 6737 5500, www.tangs.com)*, a sublime department store, sports a distinctive pagoda roof. The basement **Tangs Home** is brimming with contemporary Asian homeware and furnishings, plus great food stalls. All the top designers are here, as well as women's designer labels like **Martina Pink**, women's bags by Bonia, Perllini and Capelli, jewellery by **Kenji,** men's urban fashions from DKNY Men, IMX, funky local design label **Desigual** and the street styles of Urban Stranger.

**Touring Tip**

Orchard Road is the centre of the **Great Singapore Sale** *(May–Jul)*, when locals gather for supreme bargain-hunting. Everything here is air-conditioned and in case of heavy rain and humidity, there's no need to step outside. To keep your strength up, refuel at a food court; most malls have decent ones. Many malls are closed Chinese New Year and December 25.

**The Centrepoint** *(176 Orchard Road, daily 10am–10pm, 6737 9000, www.thecentrepoint.com.sg)* is best known for its much-loved department store **Robinsons**, supermarket **Cold Storage** (with a wonderful selection of pre-packed sushi) and British favourite **Marks and Spencer.** Come here for high-street styles from **British India**, Gap and Mango, plus gold-covered orchids at **Risis**. Overseas visitors should bring passports for assorted discounts with the Tourist Privilege Card.

**Tudor Court** *(131 Tanglin Road, hours vary)*, a row of quaint Tudor-front shops, exudes a relaxed mood for browsing, rather than high-octane shop-hopping. Try the personal touch for glamorous Indian eveningwear at **Glitterati**, Tibetan and Mongolian antiques at **Christopher Notto** and antique Chinese furniture at **The Peach Tree**. Serious collectors of valuable Tibetan antiques should browse

**Jade – Why So Precious?**

For more than 5 000 years, jade (or more specifically jadeite) has been the gem of choice in China. Its Chinese character, yu, resembles a capital I with a line across the middle, representing the heavens, earth and mankind. Emperors' tombs were clad in jade, which over time, symbolised love and virtue, and was considered a strong healing power. Although we mainly associate jade as being green, the mineral also comes in beautiful shades of translucent lavender, red-brown, blue and even black, although Imperial green is the most valuable, especially Burmese jade. With jade, you really do get what you pay for, so if you're investing in a good piece, ensure that you visit a reputable dealer.

**Antiquity**, where the owner takes his collection extremely seriously.
**Wheelock Place** *(501 Orchard Road, daily 10am–10pm, 6738 8660, www.wheelockproperties.com.sg)* is one of Orchard's most noticeable malls. The striking steel-glass conal entrance is an attraction in itself. On your way to browse books at **Borders** or have your nails done at **Snails** or a beauty treatment at **MTM Skincare**, look up through the entrance for a stunning effect, especially at night.
**Takashimaya** *(391 Orchard Road, daily 10am–9.30pm, 6738 1111, www.takashimaya-sin.com),* the red mega-Japanese department store that sits adjacent to Ngee Ann City, shows off mini-selections from top designers. Step into a bijoux **Jimmy Choo** for top footware, pick up a **Kate Spade** bag or browse the **Gift Bazaar**. Don't forget the cherished food court filled with Japanese and Chinese delicacies.
Six-level **Ngee Ann City** *(391A Orchard Road, daily 10am–9.30pm, 6733 0337, www.ngeeanncity.com.sg)* has merchandise ranging from bold Frank Gehry bangles at **Tiffany** to stylish footware at **On Pedder** and fashion from **Chanel** and other big-name designers. The mammoth Japanese **bookshop Kinokuniya** has books in all languages, Japanese comics, local history, plus a great cafe.
**The Heeren** *(260 Orchard Road, 10am–9pm, 6733 4725, www.heeren.com.sg)* features funky boutiques and home-grown designers, plus music. Its famous Level 5 boutiques have been replaced by restaurants. Level 4 provides an eclectic selection of clothes, from local designer **Benno La Mode** to shirts at **NewUrbanMale.com** and unusual hats at **Valerie**. **HMV** has a wondrous collection of contemporary, dance, local, classical and jazz, over three levels. International tourists can bring their passport to get good discounts at many stores.
**Far East Plaza** *(14 Scotts Road, daily 10am–10pm, 6734 2325, www.fareast-plaza.com)* draws local teens for low-cost quirky fashions, cult T-shirts, tattoos and piercings. For 1960s home decor and accessories, try **Attic Lifestyle Store**, and for a multi-hued selection of jeans, **New Future**. At **Tomato Can**, bags are designed in-house with a great play on the Warholian soup can. If you have a couple of weeks, get measured for a suit at top tailor **Kingsmen**. It takes much less time for a Bruce

Lee tattoo and manicure on Level 4. Feast at simple but tasty foodstalls on Level 5.

**Palais Renaissance** *(390 Orchard Road, daily 11am–8pm)* attracts Singapore's wealthy elite with its small, deluxe selection. Chic **Mumbai Se** features top designers from India, including Tarun Tahilliani, plus contemporary home furnishings and Indian artwork. **Vanilla Home** stocks a sumptuous collection of European lighting, furniture and accessories, plus ornate frames and large bars of wrapped soap. **Jim Thompson** has top silks from Thailand, with creative and exclusively designed jewellery pieces at **Yuli**.

At **Orchard Emerald** *(218 Orchard Road,daily 10am–10pm)* forget the mall. It's the market stalls outside—an Orchard Road rarity—that offer a refreshing change to top-notch designers. So make the most of outdoor browsing for scarves, cheap fun watches and last-minute gifts without having to plough through a floor plan.

**Plaza Singapura** *(68 Orchard Rd, daily 10am–10pm, 6332 9298, www.plazasingapura.com.sg)*, a nine-storey mall at the eastern end of Orchard, has a large **Times** bookstore plus a number of home furnishing stores, coffeehouses and cafés. **Made with Love** is a haven for creative teens and tweens, selling stickers, templates, patterned paper and glitter with ideas on how to create a personalised album-cover poster with photos and text.

**Wisma Atria** *(435 Orchard Road, daily 10am–10pm, 6235 8177, www.wismaonline.com)* has an excellent **Food Republic** food court on Level 4. Between it and the SISTIC ticket-booking desk on Level B1, shop at **Eclecticism** for fun boho fashions, or **Beijaflor** for bold Brazilian prints and designs, or at UK fashion chain **Dorothy Perkins**. **City Chain** stocks a collection of designer watches from Titus, Ellese, Cyma and more.

## Other Shopping Areas

Out in the suburbs, expat enclave **Holland Village** (known simply as 'Holland V') has malls with quirky clothing, plus art galleries at nearby Chip Bee Gardens.

**Katong** is best known for its Peranakan clothing and crafts in traditional shophouses.

**HarbourFront**, in sharp contrast, is the location of Singapore's largest mall, **VivoCity** *(1 HarbourFront Walk, MRT: HarbourFront, daily 10am–10pm, 6377 6870, www.vivocity.com.sg)*, which sits on the waterfront, housing **Tangs, Ted Baker, Gap** and countless others, And yes, there's a great food court on Level 3.

At this futuristic pastel-coloured mall, visitors can collect the Tourist pass for **discounts** (on presentation of passport) at the information counter on Level 1.

J. Gilbert/Michelin

*Signs in Holland Village*

# NIGHTLIFE

A night out on the town in Singapore invariably starts with dinner, followed by an evening of bar-hopping along the river, live jazz, local cinema and much more. The Cannery is a revamped area of Clarke Quay that has a covered walkway, fountains and neon lighting. Its stretch of bars, clubs and restaurants makes it a real favourite with locals. **Chijmes**, a restored Gothic chapel and convent, is now an enclave of bars, restaurants and shops. Lounge bars have sprung up at Tanglin Village (also known as Dempsey Hill), once an army barracks and now a collection of antique shops in a lush, tranquil setting. Farther out is Rochester Park, where a row of restored colonial bungalows is now home to wine bars and restaurants.

## Bars

As a general rule, most bars are open Sun–Thu 5pm–2am, Fri–Sat 5pm–3am.

### Alley Bar

*Peranakan Place Complex, 180 Orchard Road. MRT: Somerset. 6738 8818. www.peranakanplace.com.*

A long slender bar with an ornate mirror and bar stools, Alley Bar also has a VIP room with old Peranakan photos on the walls. The stylish office crowd drinks wine and bottled beer.

### Balcony Bar

*#01–K5 The Heeren, 260 Orchard Road. 6736 2326. www.balcony bar.com.*

With drapes, floor cushions and deep sofas, this bar café, open 24hrs daily, provides a good break from Orchard Road shopping, or a pre-sunrise end to a night out. Sofas, Jacuzzi and hanging basket chairs are a quirky accompaniment to the nouveau Moroccan menu.

### Bar Opiume

*Asian Civilisations Museum, 1 Empress Place. MRT: Clarke Quay. 6339 2876. www.indochine.com.sg.*

Choose between the sublime waterfront setting overlooking Boat Quay at a quiet table on weeknights, or join sophisticated locals draped over sofas to sip Prosecco at weekends. The venue of choice for high-profile events like MTV Asia post-award parties, so keep your eyes peeled for celebs.

**Getting Your Bearings**

For local listings for the city, check out **The Straits Times**, which features theatres, cinemas and concerts. The monthly magazine **Time Out Singapore** is available at newsagents and Singapore Visitor Centres, with information on regular nights, bars, clubs and gigs. **I-S** is a free fortnightly paper *(www.aziacity.com/sg)* with gig listings and features and is found at cafés, bars and bookshops. While many bars and clubs have live bands, buy tickets for major events through **SISTIC** *(6348 5555; www.sistic.com)* and outlets city-wide.

Bar Opiume

IndoChine Group

### Blu Jaz Cafe

*11 Bali Lane, Kampong Glam. MRT: Bugis. 6292 3800. www.blujaz.net.*

This is one of the few bars in Kampong Glam. Have a drink in the simple Level 1 terrace or the restaurant, or nip up to Level 3 for floor cushions and quirky decor, cool murals and jam sessions with local bands.

### China One

*Block 3E, #02–01 Clarke Quay, River Valley Road. 6339 0280. www.chinaone.com.sg.*

A deluxe pool hall in two slinky halves, China One has antique Chinese furniture, cosy nooks and pool tables, as well as day beds and a sumptuous food menu. Lots of leather chairs throughout.

### Cuba Libre

*Block B, #01–13 Clarke Quay, River Valley Road. MRT: Clarke Quay. 6338 8982. www.cubalibre.com.sg.*

Live Latin and salsa *(Tue–Sat, from Barrio Latino)* accompanies Cuban-inspired cocktails and tapas, complete with a wrought-iron Ché mural. Great Red Bull mojitos.

### Cuscaden

*#B1–11 Ming Arcade, 21 Cuscaden Road. MRT: Orchard, then taxi. Open from 3pm; closing times vary. 6887 3319.*

A real hidden gem with a tiny sunken patio and some of the cheapest beer in town. Great chicken wings, pool table and a friendly crowd.

### dbl O

*11 Unity Street, #01–24 Robertson Walk. MRT: Clarke Quay. 6735 2008. www.dbl-o.com.*

A pink neon stairway leads to this fun club, with pool tables and sofas. Weeknights are quieter, with club nights *(Wed–Sat)* drawing in the crowds for R&B and house music.

### The Dubliner

*165 Penang Road. 6735 2220. www.dublinersingapore.com.*

Decent pub food is served in this traditional Irish bar in a restored Colonial house. Pool tables, Guinness pie, live music and sports on TV make it popular at weekends.

**Taxi!**

If you're planning to grab a taxi shortly before midnight, bear in mind that the night rate (50 percent surcharge) begins at 12am. For that reason, taxi drivers tend to be thin on the ground between 11.45pm and the bewitching hour, seemingly reluctant to pick up new rides and preferring to take a break. Timing is everything!

### Giraffe

*Istana, Orchard Road. MRT: Dhoby Ghaut. Open Sun–Thu 11am–11pm, Fri–Sat 11am–1am. 6334 4653.*

Colourful sofas on the balcony and decking make Giraffe a perfect spot to relax in the midst of the city. Reasonably priced wines and bar food; reservations possible for outdoor seating (even the coveted sofas).

### Highlander

*Block 3B, The Foundry, #01–11 Clarke Quay, River Valley Road. MRT: Clarke Quay. 6235 9528. www.highlander asia.com.*

A combination of kitsch and classy, this Scottish-themed lounge bar comes complete with top malt whiskies and a menu loaded with haggis and kippers.

### Ice Cold Beer

*9 Emerald Hill Road. MRT: Somerset. 6735 9929. www.emeraldhill group.com.*

One of Emerald Hill's most relaxed bars features more than 50 varieties of bottled beers that really are served ice cold. Pool tables, dart board, cosy terrace and bar food make this an area favourite, with special promotions every night.

### Loof

*#03–07, 331 North Bridge Road. MRT: City Hall. 6338 8035. www.loof.com.sg.*

Laid-back leafy rooftop bar attracting a fun local thirtysomething crowd. The bar overlooks Raffles Hotel, and has deep leather sofas, a few cosy snugs and occasional live music. Try the white chocolate martini.

### Martini Bar

*Grand Hyatt Hotel, 10 Scotts Road. MRT: Orchard. 6732 1234. http://singapore.grand.hyatt.com.*

True to its name, the Martini Bar reputedly has Singapore's largest selection of martinis, all served in a glass-enclosed space. A stylish way to start the evening, snug in the Grand Hyatt's plush restaurant Mezza9, overlooking Scotts Road.

### Moonstone

*The Jewel Box complex,109 Mount Faber Road. MRT: HarbourFront then taxi, or cable car. 6377 9688. www.mountfaber.com.sg.*

One of several restaurants that are part of The Jewel Box on Mount Faber, this outdoor venue has staggering views of the cable car and Sentosa. It's the perfect place on a warm evening to enjoy a cocktail, and especially romantic on a starry night.

### Morton's Atrium Bar

*Hotel Mandarin Oriental, 5 Raffles Avenue, Marina Square. MRT: City Hall then walk. 6339 3740. www.mandarinoriental.com.*

At Morton's, part of the plush steakhouse, sample free steak sandwiches during busy happy hour to the sounds of cool Sinatra sounds and the mixing of martinis.

### New Asia Bar

*Level 71 & 72, Equinox Complex, Swissotel The Stamford, 2 Stamford Road. MRT: City Hall. Assorted cover charges. 6837 3322. www.equinoxcomplex.com.*

People come to this penthouse bar to perch at the window and admire the views— if you can get a window seat. Come at sunset (be prepared to pay a cover charge) for a happy hour ***lycheetini*** and gaze away.

### No. 5 Emerald Hill

*5 Emerald Hill Road. MRT: Somerset. 6732 0818. www.emeraldhillgroup.com.*

The first of the Emerald Hill bars, No. 5 has a cocktail list that is divine, and good bar food. Teak carvings adorn the walls, and Persian carpets soften your feet while you play pool upstairs. The terrace is a popular place to watch the world go by.

### One Rochester

*1 Rochester Park. MRT: Buona Vista. 6773 0070. www.onerochester.com.*

One of four colonial bungalows in lush Rochester Park, this gastro pub has several highlights: sofas in its secluded garden, a vast wine list, and the sound of crickets on warm nights.

### Oosh

*22 Dempsey Road. MRT: Orchard then taxi. 6475 0002. www.oosh.com.sg.*

Leafy and romantic, this lush bar in Dempsey (also known as Tanglin Village) has the luxury of a spacious garden with tables, plus a trellis balcony, giving you a feeling of privacy while you knock back their lychee mojitos.

### Outdoors Café & Bar

*Peranakan Place, 180 Orchard Road. MRT: Somerset. Open Sun–Thu 11am–2am, Fri–Sat 11am–3am. Happy hour 11am–7pm daily. 6738 8898.*

Rouge (the club) closed in Jan 2008, and is now tranformed into a huge patio bar with a great location on Emerald Hill. Good for a daytime pick-me-up with food. Evenings are for people-watching with a cold beer.

### The Pump Room

*#01–09 The Foundry, 3B River Valley Road, Clarke Quay. MRT: Clarke Quay. 6334 2628. www.pumproom asia.com.*

Clarke Quay's only microbrewery is a must for fans of unadulterated,

**Nightlife, Peranakan Style**

The restored Peranakan shophouses on **Emerald Hill** have become a focal point on Singapore's nightlife trail. They tend to house simple bars and restaurants in order to retain the beauty of the architecture and Old-World charm of this now preserved area. Most have a patio for alfresco imbibing, where the grace and history of the buildings can be appreciated. With live music at the **Alley Bar**, tapas in a Spanish-style ambience at **Que Pasa** and cold beer and pool tables at **Ice Cold Beer,** it might be hard to leave Emerald Hill once you start your evening.

Singapore Sling, Raffles Hotel

J. Gilbert/Michelin

real beer. It's also a civilised bistro that offers brewery tours. Bands play popular covers Tue–Sun from 10.30pm, but the place opens daily at noon (11:30am Sun).

**Que Pasa**

*7 Emerald Hill Rd. MRT: Somerset. 6235 6626. www.emeraldhill group.com.*

Top wines and tapas menu for casual dining. Interior is darkened with rough brick walls and wine bottles; upstairs has the feel of an elegant drawing room. Very popular.

**Raffles Courtyard**

*Raffles Hotel, 1 Beach Road. MRT: City Hall. 6412 1816. www.raffleshotel.com.*

A decadent alfresco cocktail bar at Singapore's hotel *par excellence*, in its colonial-style courtyard adorned with tropical palms and gorgeous balconies. A consolation for those not sleeping there. Try its famous **Singapore Sling**.

**Red Dot Brewhouse**

*25A #01–01 Dempsey Road. MRT: Orchard then taxi. 6475 0500. www.reddotbrewhouse.com.sg.*

In the tree-filled Dempsey enclave, this new microbrewery has a wide range of its own beers, accompanied by a barbecue on the terrace, perfect for Sunday lunch.

**Rupee Room**

*#01–15 Clarke Quay, 3B River Valley Road. MRT: Clarke Quay. 6334 2455. www.harrys.com.sg.*

Purple-hued lounge bar with ferocious air-conditioning, warming up with Bollywood-inspired dance music and bhangra

Red Dot Brewhouse, Dempsey Hill

**Football Fans, Rejoice!**

If you're a fan of English football, then Singapore is the perfect place for Saturday and Sunday nights out. The time difference back home, combined with Singaporeans' love of the English Premier League, means that you'll be spoilt for choice. Most bars and clubs have TV or plasma screens showing live matches, so while you're dancing, drinking and partying, you can keep one eye on the screens for live coverage of every afternoon and evening match being played in England. It can be past midnight and the dance floor is filling up, but the hard-core football fans will be watching the match draw to a close back in England. Locals here love the Big Four teams of Arsenal, Manchester Utd, Liverpool and Chelsea, and the usual banter flies just like in any bar in England.

from the DJs. Indian fusion menu and good deals on drinks.

### Tasting Notes

*#01–05/06 The Pier at Robertson, 80 Mohamed Sultan Road. www.tastingnotes.com.sg.*

A quiet venue for wine tasting, with a choice of a smooth lounge or outdoor terrace, where you can buy your favourite bottle at a discounted price.

### Wala Wala Cafe Bar

*31 Lorong Mambong, Holland Village. MRT: Holland Village. 6462 4288. www.imaginings.com.sg.*

Friendly informal neighbourhood bar, with breezy patio and upstairs stage with decent live bands every night. Tasty bar snacks.

## Nightclubs

Dress code for clubs is smart, and strictly adhered to by discerning doormen, so leave the bermuda shorts in the hotel. For those clubs with a cover charge, the price includes at least one standard drink. Cover charges vary wildly depending on which night of the week, ranging from free to S$30 for guys at weekends (usually less for women).

### The Butter Factory

*One Fullerton, 1 Fullerton Road. MRT: Raffles Place then walk. 6333 8243. www.thebutterfactory.com.*

**Happy Hours Indeed**

To compensate for Singapore's pricey drinks, most bars have their all-important Happy Hours. Timed to entice an after-work crowd for two-for-one drinks (5pm–9pm, for example), many run a second, later shift around midnight to keep you in there until the wee hours of the morning. Ladies Night is also a prominent nightlife theme in many venues, usually on Wednesdays. These high-octane nights offer free house spirits or even champagne (read inferior sparkling wine) for women. Be warned: getting to the bar is challenging, and things get raucous when revellers start dancing on the bar. It's your decision as to whether it's worth it.

**Sentosa nightlife**

Look for parties at **Azzura Beach Club**, nightclubs on Festival Walk and flow riding set to music from international DJs at **Wave House**.

For late night gambling, seek out Resorts World (*see p94*). While you are there, check out **Voyage de la Vie**, a theatrical rock circus spectacular, which celebrates Singapore's East meets West personality.

A funky, mural-filled interior by local artists, with a fun-loving crowd rather than fashion victims. Music favours soulful funk and R&B, in two separate spaces with different DJs. Regular drinks promotions.

### St. James Power Station

*3 Sentosa Gateway. MRT: HarbourFront. Cover S$10–S$20. 6270 7676. www.stjames powerstation.com.*

One ticket for entry into 12 venues housed in an old power station, from top Chinese bands in Dragonfly, Middle Eastern rhythms at Movida or R&B DJs in The Boiler Room. Good choice for global music fans.

###  Zirca

*Block 3C, The Cannery, River Valley Road, Clarke Quay. MRT: Somerset. Cover S$12–S$25. 6235 2292. www.the-cannery.com.sg.*

Formerly the Ministry of Sound, this mega-club continues to be a big hit, now as Zirca. DJ nights include hip-hop, dirty house and 80s retro, plus top international guest DJs. Over two levels, with pockets of contrasting decor, atmosphere and music.

### Zouk

*17 Jiak Kim Street. Open Wed, Fri–Sat 9pm–late, wine bar open nightly. Cover S$12–S$28. 6738 2988. www.zoukclub.com.*

Firmly on the world nightclub map since opening in 1991, Zouk offers separate venues, all sleek and uber-chic. The main club area sees top DJs spinning deep house and dance, plus futuristic decor in Phuture with breaks and nu-jazz, intimate club space Velvet and laid-back drinks in Wine Bar. A serious clubbers' mecca.

## Live Music – Rock/Jazz

Instead of high-octane nightclubs, many locals prefer a more casual evening with live music in bars. Most of Singapore's live music is based on "safe" cover versions and popular tracks. Many venues have the same opening hours as regular bars, and none have cover charges, unless stated. Jazz is also a huge

Busy nightlife along Boat Quay

favourite, with the famous Harry's Bar setting the standard.

### Acid Bar

*Peranakan Place Complex, 180 Orchard Road. MRT: Somerset. 6738 8828. www.peranakanplace.com.*

The standard of live music here is high, with several acoustic sessions nightly in this restored shophouse. Happy hour daily 5pm–9pm. Lively at weekends.

### Crazy Elephant

*3E River Valley Road, Clarke Quay. MRT: Clarke Quay. 6337 7859. www.crazyelephant.com.*

Informal timber decor and graffiti match the mood here, with blues bands playing nightly and open-mike jam session every Sunday. Burgers and pizzas on the menu.

### Hacienda

*13A Dempsey Road. MRT: Orchard then taxi. 6476 2922. www.hacienda.com.sg.*

Cool lounge singers perform from 10:30pm nightly in this plush lounge bar and veranda, with pale wood interior and sofas and adjacent garden in Dempsey's lush surrounds. This place makes a good weekend retreat.

### Harry's @ Boat Quay

*28 Boat Quay. MRT: Raffles Place. 6538 3029. www.harrys.com.sg.*

One of Boat Quay's main music spots, and first in the Harry's chain, this famous jazz landmark packs in the well-heeled professionals listening to excellent nightly live bands along the waterfront.

### Insomnia

*#01–21 Chjimes, 30 Victoria Street. MRT: City Hall. 6338 6883. www.liverockmusic247.com.*

Live cover bands ***(nightly, until 4am)*** perform popular rock and chart music in the converted medieval chapel grounds. If that gets too much, slip out to the huge courtyard for a cool beer.

### Jazz @ Southbridge

*82B Boat Quay. MRT: Clarke Quay. 6327 4671. www.southbridgejazz.com.sg.*

This friendly bar hosts musicians six nights a week, with occasional international jazz stars. The venue for serious jazz fans, with tables for relaxed listening. Happy hour Tue–Sat 5pm–9pm.

### Prince of Wales

*101 Dunlop Street, Little India. MRT: Little India. 6299 0130. www.pow.com.sg.*

A different band every night plays from around 9pm in this down-to-earth fun bar, which is part of a backpackers hostel with a garden and plenty of Australian beers. One of the few bars in Little India.

### Timbre @ The Arts House

*#01–04, 1 Old Parliament Lane. MRT: City Hall. Open from 6pm. 6336 3386. www.timbre.com.sg.*

Relax on the huge deck overlooking Boat Quay, with live music from a core of Singaporean bands, from blues to rock. Great pizzas and a good wine list.

# SPAS

Singapore's spa industry has blossomed in luxury hotels, resorts and independent salons, including some in restored shophouses and colonial-era bungalows. Spa treatments range from Thai and **Balinese massages** to Ayuverdic treatments and traditional Chinese foot reflexologies. A one-hour massage costs about S$100.

## Kenko Wellness Spa

*199 South Bridge Road. MRT: Chinatown. 6223 0303. www.kenko.com.sg.*

Part of a popular chain of foot **reflexology** centres and spas, this outlet, located in a two-storey shophouse, has a modern setting that is clean and pleasant. Foot therapies include reflexology, foot bath and foot spa. Body and beauty treatments also available.

## Eucalyptus Day Spa

*43A Craig Road. MRT: Tanjong Pagar. 6324 1338. www.eucalyptus.com.sg.*

Nestled in a quaint 100-year-old shophouse, Eucalyptus Day Spa offers a tranquil ambience and an open-air rooftop garden. The spa's treatments are derived from central and east Asian techniques, and include the Egyptian massage, Ayurvedic therapy, and exotic body scrubs and mud wraps.

## The Aspara at Amara Singapore

*The Amara Singapore Hotel, Level 6. 165 Tanjong Pagar Road. MRT: Tanjong Pagar. 6879 2688. www.aspara.com.sg.*

Traditional and contemporary treatments mostly use in-house products such as aromatic massage oils and exfoliating sugar scrubs specially created by the spa team. Book the exotic Indonesian Body Massage, Fragrant Flower Bath, or more generic Detoxifying Seaweed Body Mask and Hydrotherapy Bath. Spa suites feature a theme, such as the Balinese-inspired Amaryllis Spa Suite for a resort feel, or the Orchid Spa Suite, which boasts an Oriental vibe.

## The Oriental Spa

*The Mandarin Oriental Hotel, Level 5. 5 Raffles Avenue, Marina Square. MRT: City Hall. 6885 3533. www.mandarinoriental.com.*

Using pure essential oils and herbs, the swanky Oriental Spa's restorative treatments combine both ancient and modern techniques and philosophies. The spa comprises four luxurious treatment rooms, a couples' suite, a shiatsu room, a private relaxation lounge, a mind and body yoga studio and a high-performance exercise studio.

## Ayurlly Ayurvedic Spa

*2 Serangoon Road, #05-11/13 Tekka Mall. MRT: Little India. 6737 5657. www.ayurlly.com.*

Holistic Ayurvedic treatments include the *Shirodhara* (stress-relieving oil treatment), an ancient calming therapy to rejuvenate the scalp and hair. The therapist pours medicated warm oil in a constant stream to the midpoint on the forehead ("third eye") and follows this up with a massage. Another signature treatment is the ***Sheeradhara*** (stress-relieving milk treatment), where cooling medicated milk is poured in the same manner to relieve tension, sleeplessness and giddiness.

## St. Gregory Spa

*Parkroyal on Beach Road, Level 4, 7500 Beach Road, 6505 5755. www.stgregoryspa.com.*

Set within a leafy tropical Balinese-inspired garden, the St. Gregory draws its treatments from the Indonesian islands. Spa services range from Balinese massage, and Javanese ***Lulur*** (a saffron-based body scrub that's traditionally reserved for Javanese royalty) to the ***Mandi Kepala*** (a hair crème bath treatment that moisturises the hair and scalp and relaxes the body).

## ESTHEVA Spa

*ION Orchard Mall. MRT: Orchard. 6733 9300. www.estheva.com.*

One of Singapore's most exclusive and lavish women-only spas has relocated to the new ION Orchard Mall. ESTHEVA's relaxing range of beauty treatments includes anti-aging therapies, bodyworks and massages. Try the Chocolatier's Massage (using pure warm chocolate), part of the exotic signature Choc De-Ager Spa treatment.

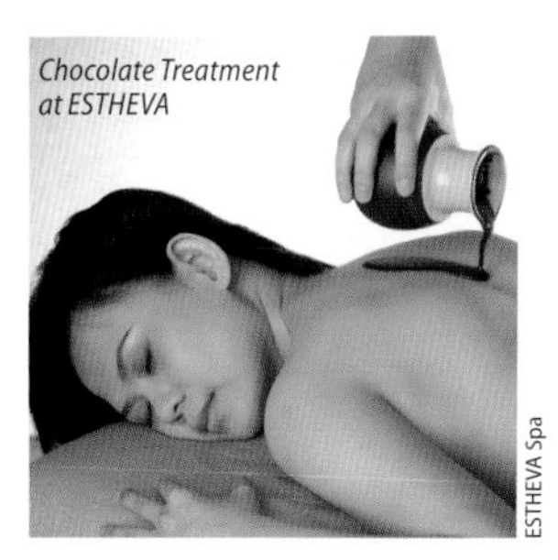

*Chocolate Treatment at ESTHEVA*

ESTHEVA Spa

## SK-II Boutique Spa

*31 Scotts Road. MRT: Newton. 6836 9168. www.senzesalus.com.*

Housed in a colonial black-and-white bungalow, this spa offers a full range of SK-II facials and spa services such as body massages and polishes using the brand's pitera-based products.

## Spa Esprit at House

*8D Dempsey Road. 6479 0070. www.dempseyhouse.com/ www.spa-esprit.com.*

Located in converted military barracks, this day spa offers treatments sourced from different countries. Unique treatments include the Mud Stones Massage, Cheeky Chai Detox, Strawberry Butter Meltdown, and Crystal Tonic Facials. Follow up with a stroll around the gardens or enjoy one of 50 specially blended herbal teas.

## Spaboutique

*6 Nassim Road. MRT: Orchard. 6887 0760. www.spaboutique.com.sg.*

Located in an early 20C colonial-style bungalow, this boutique is a home-style spa set in lush greenery. Personalised touches greet clients at every turn, including day beds, vanity tables and bookshelves. The unusual Thai Five Spice body wrap infuses nutmeg, cinnamon, ginger, turmeric and lemongrass with crushed rice.

# RESTAURANTS

For a tiny island, Singapore's multicultural dining scene offers a mind-boggling spread of dining options and two food festivals, the World Gourmet Summit *(Apr)* and the Singapore Food Festival *(Jul)*. From refined Japanese and robust Italian meals to casual French bistro and classic northern Indian fare, Singapore has it all. Whether it's fine dining or open-air hawker centres, there's an eatery at almost every turn.

## Prices and Amenities

The restaurants below were selected for their ambience, location, variety of regional dishes and/or value for money. Prices indicate the average cost of an appetizer, entrée and dessert for one person, not including taxes or beverages. Most restaurants are open daily (except where noted) but many don't serve lunch Saturdays. Not all accept major credit cards.

| | |
|---|---|
| **$** | <S$25 |
| **$$** | S$25 to 50 |
| **$$$** | S$50 to 75 |
| **$$$$** | >S$75 |

## Cuisine

Given that Indian and Chinese immigrant communities always set up restaurants wherever they go, Singapore has gained a particularly rich culinary heritage. National dishes that have survived intact and fusion dishes that have been adapted to Singaporean tastes both serve as metaphors for the cultural mix of this island. People in Little India queue for ***thalis***, south Indian vegetarian food traditionally served on banana leaves. In Chinatown the Hokkien origins of many early immigrants to Singapore are reflected in ***Hokkien mee*** (fried noodles brought by immigrants from China's Fujian Province) as well as ***luak*** (oyster omelette) and ***popiah*** (spring rolls). Cantonese settlers brought dim sum to Singapore while chicken rice came from Hainan island and Peking Duck from Beijing.

*Hainanese chicken rice*

©Singapore Tourism Board

## Must-Try Dishes

**Bak kut teh** – Literally "pork bone tea", this Singaporean and Malaysian soup consists of meaty pork ribs in a broth of herbs and spices (including star anise, cinnamon, cloves, ***dang gui*** and garlic) boiled together with pork bones for hours. A popular morning dish, it is usually eaten with rice and often served with ***youtiao*** (strips of fried dough) for dipping into the soup.

**Char Kway Teow** – "Fried flat noodles" is a popular staple of Malaysia and Singapore. Created as a budget meal full of energy and nutrients for labourers, the dish is high in fat and cheap to prepare.

**Chicken Rice** – Immigrants from China's Hainan island introduced chicken rice to Singapore many decades ago. Today it is an iconic dish adored by all. Velvety

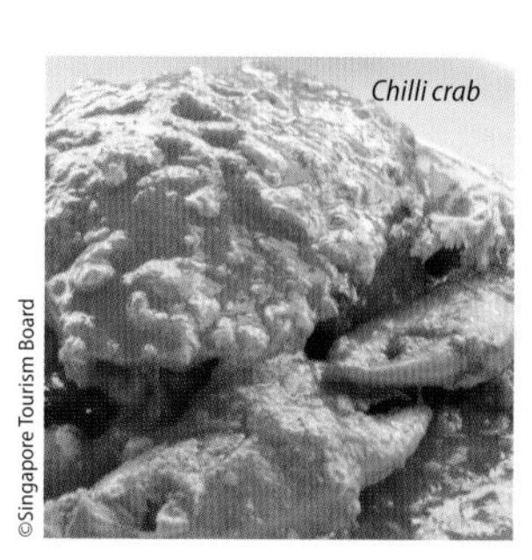
Chilli crab



poached chicken is partnered with fragrant rice cooked in chicken broth with ginger and garlic. The dish is usually accompanied by zesty chilli-lime sauce, pungent ginger paste, and black soy sauce.

**Chilli Crab** – Sweet and juicy Sri Lankan crabs are used for this unofficial "national" dish. The crustaceans are doused with a rich gravy, and often jazzed up with spices like galangal, ginger and turmeric, spiked with chilli oil, coloured with tomatoes or ribboned with beaten egg. The delicious tangy gravy is mopped up with deep-fried *mantou* (soft Chinese buns) or baguette slices.
The black pepper version is spiced up with plenty of crushed peppercorn, and has less gravy.

**Fish Head Curry** – Served at various Indian restaurants, large fish heads are simmered in a spicy gravy with okra, tomatoes and aubergines. Some diners zero in on the meaty cheeks, lips and eyes.

**Ketupat** – For these dumplings, rice is wrapped in a woven palm leaf pouch, which is then boiled; the grains expand to fill the pouch, which compresses the mix. *Ketupat* is usually eaten with *rendang* (a type of dry beef curry) or served as an accompaniment to *satay*, usually on festive occasions.

**Laksa** –Spicy and ever-popular, this noodle soup is a Peranakan dish also found in Malaysia's mixed Chinese/Malay families.

**Popiah** – A thin flour crepe is daubed with chilli paste and a dark caramel sauce, then topped with lettuce, and *bangkwang* (a turnip-like root) braised with bamboo shoots, salted soybean paste, pork and prawns. The rolled up crepe is garnished with chopped hard-boiled eggs, prawns, beansprouts, cucumber and coriander leaves.

**Roti Prata** – The Singaporean version of the Indian *paratha*, this pancake made of fat, egg, flour and water is normally served with curry, sugar, or condensed milk and usually eaten as a midnight snack or early in the morning.

**Satay** – One of the earliest local foods associated with Singapore, satays look sort of like a shish kebab—they are meat on a stick. Slices of marinated meat, chicken or fish are barbecued or grilled on a bamboo or other type of skewer, and served with a peanut dipping sauce. The most popular *satays* are *satay ayam* (chicken), *satay lembu* (beef), *satay kambing* (mutton), *satay perut* (beef intestine) and *satay babat* (beef tripe).

Laksa

J. Gilbert/Michelin

*Grilling satay, Lau Pa Sat Hawker Centre*

## CBD

### $ Lau Pa Sat Festival Market

*Corner of Boon Tat Street and Robinson Road. MRT: Raffles Place.*

The name means "old market" in Chinese, and the entire building (the largest remaining Victorian filigree cast-iron structure in Southeast Asia) is an 1894 landmark. Its bewildering spread of stalls, set in the heart of the financial district, offer hawker dishes around the clock. **Hawker Centre**

## CHINATOWN

## Centre

### $ Amoy Street Hawker Centre

*Corner of Telok Ayer and Amoy Street. MRT: Tanjong Pagar.*

Located near the Thian Hock Keng Temple, this is a great place for Chinese favourites such as Teochew minced-meat noodles, a dish that combines al dente noodles with a chilli-vinegar-shallot oil sauce and tender minced pork. **Chinese Hawker Centre**.

### $ Maxwell Food Centre

*MRT: Chinatown.*

This food haven has been around for more than six decades. It is jammed-packed with office workers during lunch, so consider visiting in the evening when it's cooler and considerably less crowded. There are more than 100 food stalls offering a superb range of dishes. **Hawker Centre**.

### $$ 25 Degree Celsius

*25 Keong Saik Road, #01–01. MRT: Outram Park. 6327 8389. www.25degreec.com.*

The tiny kitchen of this café-cookbook store serves up hearty salads and paninis. End the meal with a sticky date pudding. **Fusion**.

### $$ Beng Hiang

*112-116 Amoy Street. MRT: Raffles Place. 6221 6695. www.benghiang.com.*

At this authentic Hokkien restaurant, dig into fish flavoured with ginger and vinegar, ***kong bak*** or fatty pork belly, flavoured with garlic and soy sauce, and fried ***bee hoon*** (rice vermicelli) with prawns. **Chinese**.

### $$ Ka Soh

*96 Amoy Street. MRT: Tanjong Pagar. 6224 9920. www.ka-soh.com.sg.*

Ka Soh's homely Cantonese classics are served by stern but motherly staff. Best sellers include delicious deep-fried chicken marinated in prawn paste, deep-fried cubes of lightly salted tofu, and a milky, fish head *bee hoon* noodle soup. **Chinese**.

### $$ Spring Court

*52–56 Upper Cross Street. MRT: Chinatown. 6449 5030. www.springcourt.com.sg.*

Though it's moved since opening in 1929, the family-run Spring Court is looking swanky in its latest location. The oldest Chinese restaurant in Singapore dishes out Singaporean Cantonese cuisine. **Chinese**.

### $$ Tiffin Club

*16 Jiak Chuan Road. MRT: Outram Park. 6323 3189. www.thetiffinclub.com.*

This tucked-away eatery serves excellent comfort fare. The daily specials focus on Sri Lankan curries. Also on offer are sweet treats. Breakfast is available all day. **Western and Asian**.

### $$ Whatever Café

*20 Keong Saik Road. MRT: Outram. 6224 0300. www.whatever.com.sg.*

Chic yet understated, Whatever parlays its laidback vibe into a wholesome organic vegetarian menu. Also on offer is a mix of guilt-free wheat/gluten/dairy/egg or sugar-free cakes and pastries that are delicious. **Western**.

### $$$ Desire

*The Scarlet Hotel, 33 Erskine Road. MRT: Chinatown. 6511 3323. www.thescarlethotel.com.*

Chef Vincent Teng, formerly of My Dining Room, has introduced menus of simple, modern flavours. Must-tries include the cheese tartlet and the wonderful Kurobuta pork. **Modern European**.

### $$$ Ember

*Hotel 1929, Ground Floor, 50 Keong Saik Road. MRT: Outram Park/ Chinatown. 6347 1929. www.hotel1929.com.*

Chef Sebastian Ng's modern menu is a mix of Western and Asian ingredients. Enjoy the pan-seared scallops with Parma ham and an orange and tarragon vinaigrette. **Fusion**.

### $$$ Seven on Club

*7 Club Street. MRT: Chinatown. 6327 9663.*

Mediterranean cuisine meets South American via a partnership with Sixth Avenue stalwart Brazil Churrascaria. The highlight is the churrascaria: the waiter cuts slices from the grilled lamb, beef, chicken and pork skewers directly onto plates. **Mediterranean**.

## Club Street

### $$ Spizza

*29 Club Street. MRT: Raffles Place. 6224 2525. www.spizza.sg.*

Spizza stands out from other pizza joints mainly because of its insistence on authentic thin-crusted pizzas made à la minute in its wood-fired oven using fresh ingredients. **Italian**.

### $$$ Screening Room

*12 Ann Siang Road. MRT: Tanjong Pagar. 6221 1694. www.screenroom.com.sg.*

Restaurateur Samia Ahad transformed a run-down backpackers' hotel into the five-storey Screening Room—an up-scale film-based

dining experience comprising a restaurant, bars and movie theatres. Dine, then head upstairs to watch classic films like *Babette's Feast* and *Eat Drink Man Woman*, followed by drinks at the rooftop bar. **Mediterranean**.

### $$$$ Senso Ristorante & Bar

*21 Club Street. MRT: Raffles Place. 6224 3534. www.senso.sg.*

Dine in the interior hall or in the inviting courtyard at this former convent. The set dinner menu is inspired by specific regions of Italy such as Lazio, Tuscany and Piedmont and is changed monthly. There's even a walk-in wine cellar. **Italian**.

## Tanjong Pagar

### $$ The Blue Ginger

*97 Tanjong Pagar Road. MRT: Tanjong Pagar. 6222 3928. www.theblueginger.com.*

For more than a decade now, The Blue Ginger has been preparing delicious and authentic Peranakan cuisine. House specialities include *ayam panggang,* or grilled chicken flavoured with coconut milk and spices, and *chap chye masak titek*, a mixed vegetable dish prepared in an intense prawn stock. **Peranakan**.

### $$$ Broth

*21 Duxton Hill. MRT: Tanjong Pagar. 6323 3353. www.broth.com.sg. Closed Sun.*

Walk up a cobble-stoned slope to a row of colonial period shophouses and Broth (charmingly short for Bar/Restaurant on the Hill). Here, chef-owner Steven Hansen presides over a menu of hearty and often innovative food. **Australian**.

### $$$ Buko Nero

*126 Tanjong Pagar Road. MRT: Tanjong Pagar. 6324 6225.*

Chef Oscar Pasinato and his wife Tracy run the incredibly popular, tiny 20-seater Buko Nero. Reservations several weeks in advance are standard. **Italian-Asian**.

### $$$ Pasta Brava

*11 Craig Road. MRT: Tanjong Pagar. 6227 7550. www. pastabrava.com. Closed Sun.*

The rustic and warm decor in this old shophouse is reminiscent of a home-spun restaurant in Italy. The chef-owner pulls out all the stops to ensure guests feel at home. Antipasti, homemade pastas and pumpkin-filled ravioli. **Italian**.

### $$$$ Xi Yan

*38A Craig Road. MRT: Tanjong Pagar. 6220 3546. www.xiyan.com.sg.*

With barely six tables, Xi Yan is the sole overseas outlet of the famed private-kitchen restaurant in Hong Kong. Graphic-designer-turned-chef Jacky Yu's multiple-course degustation menu offers bold Asian flavours. Reservations are required **Chinese**.

## Riverside Point (across the river from Clarke Quay)

### $ Red Star

*#07–23, Block 54 Chin Swee Road. MRT: Chinatown. 6532 5266.*

This popular restaurant has loyal followers who know they won't be disappointed by the ***char siew*** (barbecued pork and roast goose), the ***siew mai*** (steamed pork and shrimp dumplings) and other dim sum dishes. But you'll be disappointed if you have to wait for a table, so better to arrive early, especially on weekends. **Chinese**.

### $$ Brewerkz

*30 Merchant Road, #01–05/06 Riverside Point. MRT: Clarke Quay. 6438 7438. www.brewerkz.com.*

Brewerkz is a popular microbrewery and restaurant. The focus here is on hearty American-style food from the Deep South, the Southwest and California, all paired with a yeasty range of premium beers handcrafted on-site. **American**.

### $$ Café Iguana

*30 Merchant Road, #01–03 Riverside Point. MRT: Clarke Quay. 6236 1275. www.cafeiguana.com. Brunch Sat–Sun noon–4pm.*

The lively Café Iguana is perpetually packed, thanks to its delicious tortillas, salsas and guacamole, and more than100 kinds of 100 percent blue agave tequila and handcrafted mescal (Mexican distilled spirit made from agave). **Tex Mex**.

### $$ Wine Garage

*30 Merchant Road, #01–07 Riverside Point. MRT: Clarke Quay. 6533 3188. www.winegarage.com.sg.*

Just across the river from Clarke Quay, this narrow restaurant and wine bar is lovely during balmy evenings. The wines are excellent, service is efficient and friendly and the food utterly satisfying. Favourites include poached oysters, potato chips with blue cheese fondue, Kurobuta pork chop and lava chocolate cake. **European**.

### $$$$ Saint Pierre

*#01–01 Central Mall, 3 Magazine Road. 6438 0887. www.saintpierre.com.sg.*

With his high-rating cooking shows on TV and cookbooks, the Belgian-born Emmanuel Stroobant is the closest Singapore has to a celebrity chef. His French menu, injected with Japanese influence, is always highly innovative, and his foie gras dishes remain celebrated. **Modern French**.

## Havelock Road Area

### $ Tiong Bahru Market

*Corner of Lim Liak Street and Seng Poh Road. MRT: Tiong Bahru.*

A perennial favourite for hawker food junkies, Tiong Bahru Market was renovated a few years ago, but happily, its food remains as delicious (and cheap) as ever. Stalls sell grilled wings, fried ***kway teow***, roast duck and roast pork. **Hawker Centre**.

MUST EAT

### $$ Princess Terrace

*Copthorne King's Hotel, 403 Havelock Road.6318 3168. www.millenniumhotels.com.sg.*

For years now, the Princess Terrace's authentic Penang buffet has drawn a regular crowd who adore its irresistible spread of Penang-styled *laksa*, prawn noodles, chicken curry, and colourful, coconut infused desserts. **Penang**.

## South Chinatown

### $$ Magma

*2 Bukit Pasoh Road. MRT: Outram Park. 6221 0634. www.magmatc.com.*

The underrated Magma presents casual and nostalgic German fare. The massive pork knuckle and bratwurst are delicious. German wines are available by the glass, starting from S$9. **German**.

### $$$ Majestic

*New Majestic Hotel, First Floor, 31–37 Bukit Pasoh Road. MRT: Outram Park or Chinatown. 6511 4718. www.newmajestichotel.com.*

The small dining room in this stylish boutique hotel presents brilliant modern Chinese fare. Award-winning chef Yong Bing Ngen re-creates Cantonese classics, effortlessly turning out flash-fried prawns in wasabi sauce and lobsters baked in carnation milk. **Modern Chinese.**

### $$$ Oso

*46 Bukit Pasoh Road. MRT: Outram Park. 6327 8378. www.oso.sg. Closed Sun.*

Oso recently moved from Tanjong Pagar to Bukit Pasoh Road. Chef Diego Chiarini's mainstay is the rigatoni with a rich, muscular sauce of thyme, black olives and tender rabbit. Cheese and cold cuts are housed in a separate climate-controlled room, while the well-stocked wine cellar does double duty as a private dining room. **Italian**.

# COLONIAL DISTRICT

## Boat Quay

### $$ Molly Malone's

*56 Circular Road. MRT: Raffles Place. 6536 2029. www.molly-malone.com.*

Designed and built in Ireland, the pub was shipped to Singapore and reassembled on-site. Pair a pint with fish and chips, shepherd's pie or Irish lamb stew—and Irish music. **Irish pub grub**.

### $$$ Moomba

*52 Circular Road.  MRT: Raffles Place. 6438 0141. www.themoomba.com.*

Chef Leonard Oh wows with modern Australian cuisine. Signatures include breaded deep-fried squid cake with mango salad and tomato risotto with marinated olive leaves and gratinated oakwood smoked cheddar. **Australian**.

### $$$ Samarkand

*52 Boat Quay. MRT: Raffles Place. 6535 4222.*

North Indian fare is the specialty here, in particular the traditional cooking of the Frontier regions. Make room for aromatic kebabs and curries like fresh crabmeat masala and *saag gosht*—tender boneless mutton cooked with garlic, ginger and Indian spices, tossed in puréed spinach. **Indian**.

## Fullerton

 $$$ Jade

*The Fullerton Hotel Singapore, 1 Fullerton Square. MRT: Raffles Place. 6877 8188.*

Look forward to a sophisticated menu of Cantonese classics such as steamed squid ink dumpling stuffed with squid or shrimp and sea prawn cooked three ways: with ginger dressing, wasabi mayonnaise and crispy honey glaze. **Chinese**.

### $$$$ The Lighthouse

*The Fullerton Hotel Singapore, 8th Floor, 1 Fullerton Square. MRT: Raffles Place. 6877 8933.*

Enjoy an incredible setting on the top of the grand Fullerton Hotel with panoramic views of the harbour. The menu is injected with plenty of creativity. Don't pass up the foie gras terrine and the signature roasted crispy rack of Kurobuta piglet. **Italian**.

## Centre

### $ Brotzeit

*Raffles City Shopping Centre, Ground Floor, #01–17, 252 North Bridge Road. MRT: City Hall. 6883 1534. www.brotzeit1516.com.*

This contemporary café and bar serves up German beer and Bavarian food from noon to midnight daily. Traditional dishes include wiener schnitzel (breaded veal), tafelspitz (boiled beef), accompanied by German roasted potatoes. **German**.

### $ Sofra

*100 Beach Road, #02–42 Shaw Tower. MRT: Bugis. 6291 1433. www.sofra.com.sg.*

The ever popular Sofra's low-key Turkish menu is filled with reliable favourites at affordable prices, including platters of hummus and aubergine dips served up with crispbreads and apple tea. **Turkish**.

### $$ Asia Grand Restaurant

*#01-02 Odeon Towers, 331 North Bridge Rd. MRT: City Hall.6887 0010.*

Locals come here for the delectable Cantonese dishes, despite a decor that is hardly muted. The aubergine stir-fried with salted eggs and minced pork is one of the best versions in town. A few dim sum items are on the menu as well. **Chinese**.

### $$ A-roy Thai

*109 North Bridge Road, #04–06 Funan DigitaLife Mall. MRT: City Hall. 6338 3880.*

A-roy's non-descript interiors belie the superb quality of its kitchen. House specials include tongue burning ***tom yam*** and delicately stuffed chicken wings. **Thai**.

### $$ Empire Café

*Raffles Hotel, 1 Beach Road. MRT: City Hall. 6412 1816. www.raffles.com.*

Empire Café serves a menu of Asian classics, among them, ***nasi goreng*** (Malay fried rice), ***laksa*** noodles, chicken rice and dim sum. The prices are considerably higher than the equivalent dishes at hawker stalls, but this fact doesn't deter diners from returning for the consistently good food and charming nostalgic vibe. **Asian**.

### $$ Japanese Dining SUN

*#02–01 Chijmes, 30 Victoria Street. MRT: City Hall. 6336 3166. www.sfbi.com.sg.*

Watch chefs in action at the open kitchen while tucking into the house specials of jumping fresh sushi, sashimi and teppanyaki. The desserts are sublime. **Japanese**.

###  $$ Yhingthai Palace

*36 Purvis Street. #01-04. MRT: City Hall. 6337 1161. www.yhingthai.com.*

This Thai-Chinese restaurant has been drawing crowds here for years, and with good reason. The food is authentically prepared and consistently tasty. The fried olive rice, fish cakes and heady ***tom yam*** soups are all quite satisfying. **Thai**.

### $$$ Flutes at the Fort

*21 Lewin Terrace, Fort Canning Park. MRT City Hall. 6338 8770. www.flutesatthefort.com.sg.*

An ideal place for a romantic meal or a special occasion, Flutes charms as much for its alluring Australian cuisine as for its lovely setting in an old colonial home tucked away among Fort Canning's frangipani trees. **Modern Australian**.

### $$$ Lei Garden

*#01–24 Chijmes, 30 Victoria Street. MRT: City Hall. 6339 3822.*

A favourite among local residents, the elegant Lei Garden is one of the best venues in town for dim sum and refined Cantonese dishes. The expansive dining area is flooded with sunlight, thanks to the large windows overlooking the manicured gardens of Chijmes, a former convent. **Chinese**.

### $$$ Szechuan Court

*Level 3, Fairmont Singapore, 80 Bras Basah Road. MRT: City Hall. 6431 6156. www.fairmont.com.*

Szechuan Court features a contemporary interpretation of dishes culled from Imperial China's Szechuan and Canton provinces. From Szechuan, try the crispy diced chicken fried with dried chilli. For a refined Cantonese classic dish, the steamed marble goby in superior soy sauce is served with vegetables and wolfberries poached in a flavourful broth. **Chinese**.

### $$$ True Blue Cuisine

*49 Armenian Street.
MRT: City Hall. 6440 0449.
www.truebluecuisine.com.*

Dine on expertly crafted Peranakan classics in a charming two-storey shophouse just next to the Peranakan Museum. Standards dishes like beef ***rendang*** (a spicy beef stew) and ***ayam buah keluak*** (chicken stewed with keluak nuts) are superbly done, though a little expensive for the small portions. **Peranakan**.

### $$$$ Chef Chan's Restaurant

*#01–06 National Museum of Singapore, 93 Stamford Road.
MRT: Dhoby Ghaut. 6333 0073.
www.chefchanrestaurant.com.sg.*

Chef Chan Chen Hei relocated his restaurant and personal antique collection to a more intimate space at the National Museum. Flawlessly executed Cantonese delicacies include crispy-skinned chicken, and king prawns bathed in a broth studded with ginger, red dates and ginseng. Only set menus are available. **Chinese**.

### $$$$ Garibaldi

*#01–02, 36 Purvis Street.
MRT: City Hall. 6837 1468.
www.garibaldi.com.sg.*

Garibaldi is worth the splurge. Its sophisticated Italian menu is ably helmed by its charming chef Roberto Galetti. Only the best seasonal ingredients from Italy are used to prepare the braised veal shank with saffron risotto and the truffle and Taleggio cheese fondue. **Italian**.

### $$$$ Gunther's

*#01–03, 36 Purvis Street.
MRT: City Hall. 6338 8955.
www.gunthers.com.sg.*

Decked out with white table linens and leather chairs, Gunther's offers hushed conversations and French cuisine on big plates.The small menu is well edited to include foie gras encrusted with toasted almonds and paired with stewed sweet cherries, and tender braised rabbit with prunes, brown beer and Valrhona chocolate. **Modern French**.

### $$$$ Inagiku

*Fairmont Singapore Hotel, 3rd Floor, 80 Bras Basah Road. MRT: City Hall. 6431 6156. www.fairmont.com.*

This fine dining restaurant boasts beautifully executed Japanese dishes prepared with ingredients all air-flown in from Japan. The talented head chef is licensed to prepare the toxic fugu (puffer fish) delicacy. **Japanese**.

### $$$$ Raffles Grill

*Raffles Hotel, 1 Beach Road.
MRT: City Hall. 6412 1816.
www.singapore.raffles.com.*

Elegant and formal, the Raffles Grill's fine dining room oozes a grace not out of place with its setting in the stately Raffles Hotel. Traditional rustic French flavours are paired with quality provincial produce. The wine list is comprehensive, while the service is discreetly attentive. **French**.

MUST EAT

## Clarke Quay

### $$ Ellenborough Market Café

*Swissotel Merchant Court Hotel, 20 Merchant Road. MRT: Clarke Quay. 6239 1848.*

Overlooking Clarke Quay and the Singapore river, the Ellenborough offers relaxing dining indoors or alfresco on the terrace. The huge buffet spread presents international fare and local favourites like fried carrot cake, ***nonya laksa lemak*** with prawn, and sweet treats such as pandan crème brûlée or rum and raisin bread pudding. **Peranakan/Asian**.

### $$ Ma Maison

*#03–96 Central, 6 Eu Tong Sen Street. MRT: Clarke Quay. 6327 8122.*

With its dark timber panelling, faux Tiffany table lamps and hodgepodge of trinkets, Ma Maison is a hit. Japanese expats and locals, in particular, rave about the rice dishes, the sirloin steaks and the burgers. **Japanese/ Western**.

### $$ Peony-Jade

*Block 3A, Clarke Quay, #02–02, River Valley Road. MRT: Clarke Quay. 6338 0305/0138. www.peonyjade.com.*

Peony-Jade offers well executed, boldly flavoured traditional Szechuan cuisine. The signature Szechuan smoked duck with camphor wood and fragrant tea leaves, served with steamed Chinese flower buns, is sublime. The setting, against a languid backdrop of the Singapore river, is elegant and contemporary. **Chinese**.

### $$ Shiraz

*Block 3A River Valley Road, Clarke Quay, #01–06 Merchant Court. MRT: Clarke Quay. 6334 2282. www.shirazfnb.com.*

Shiraz's generous portions of authentic Iranian dishes could easily be shared. The braised aubergine, tomato-based lamb stew with okra, and smoky charcoal-grilled kebabs are fabulous, as are the delicious Persian desserts. **Persian**.

### $$$ Coriander Leaf

*#02–03, 3A Merchant Court, 3A River Valley Road. MRT: Clarke Quay. 6732 3354. www.corianderleaf.com.*

The pan-Asian menu is a mix of flavours from Indo-China, Persia, India and owner Samia Ahad's native Pakistan. The pilafs and lamb kebabs are fabulous with garlic naans. The charming restaurant overlooks the Singapore river, and so the best tables are by the window. **Modern European/ Asian**.

## Marina Bay

### $ Makansutra Gluttons Bay

*#01–15 Esplanade Mall, The Esplanade - Theatres on the Bay. MRT: City Hall. 6336 7025. www.makansutra.com.*

Some of the best hawker stalls in Singapore have been selected to set up shop here next to the Esplanade Mall. The oyster omelette and *char kway teow* (fried rice noodles) stalls are especially popular. **Hawker Centre**.

### $$ No Signboard Esplanade

*The Esplanade - Theatres on the Bay, 8 Raffles Avenue, #01–14. MRT: City Hall. 6336 9959. www.nosignboard seafood.com.*

Enjoy the water view at the oddly named No Signboard (one of four outlets on the island) while feasting on lip-smacking crabs fried with either a luridly spicy chilli or black pepper sauce. **Seafood**.

### $$ Paulaner Bräuhaus

*9 Raffles Boulevard, Time²@ Millenia Walk. MRT: City Hall. 6883 2572. www.paulaner.com.sg. Sunday German Brunch 11.30am–2.30pm.*

Established ten years ago, Paulaner Bräuhaus' restaurant is located on a mezzanine floor above its usually crowded bar. Complement the large mugs of freshly brewed German beer with traditional Bavarian cuisine like char-grilled Nuremberg bratwurst served on a bed of sauerkraut and mashed potatoes. **German**.

### $$ Rakuzen

*9 Raffles Boulevard, #01–14 Time²@ Millenia Walk. MRT: City Hall. 6333 1171.*

If you want to watch Rakuzen's chefs do their magic, sit at the counter; otherwise take a booth at the back. Seasonal specials are offered here daily and typically include several types of seafood or fish and fresh vegetables. You'll find that the rice is fresh as well, since it's made on the premises. Bookings are necessary especially for lunch. **Japanese**.

### $$$ Cherry Garden

*Mandarin Oriental Hotel, 5 Raffles Avenue, Marina Square. MRT: City Hall. 6885 3538. Sat–Sun Dim Sum Buffet 11am–3pm.*

The sleek Cherry Garden offers a modern menu featuring artistically presented Cantonese cuisine. The signature dish, oven-baked fillet of sea perch in spicy sesame-garlic-balsamic glaze on a bed of soy aubergine, is not to be missed. **Chinese**.

### $$$ Dolce Vita

*Mandarin Oriental Hotel, 5 Raffles Avenue, Marina Square. MRT: City Hall. 6885 3551.*

Located next to the hotel's landscaped outdoor pool, Dolce Vita is bright and breezy, and makes a perfect spot for a lazy lunch. The menu, with influences from France, Spain, Greece and Morocco, is simple and fresh. **Italian**.

### $$$ Greenhouse

*Ritz-Carlton Millenia Hotel, 7 Raffles Ave. MRT: City Hall. 6337 8888. www.ritzcarlton.com.*

A must is the popular Sunday champagne brunch, (*11.30am–3pm)* which includes free-flowing vintage Moët & Chandon, with a host of delicacies like fresh Boston lobsters, oysters, pan-fried foie gras, and more than 50 varieties of Ceneri farmhouse cheeses. **Contemporary**.

©My Humble House/Singapore Tourism Board

### $$$ My Humble House

*#02–27 The Esplanade - Theatres on the Bay. MRT: City Hall. 6423 1881. www.myhumblehouse.com.*

This restaurant always makes a splash with its outré Alice in Wonderland-inspired interiors, sexy lighting, plush oversized furniture, and extravagantly plated Neoclassic Chinese dishes. Aesthetics aside, the kitchen ensures that dishes like the crispy spiced pork rib in sun-dried tomato reduction, or the steamed fillet of cod are perfectly executed. **Chinese**.

### $$$ Rang Mahal

*Pan Pacific Hotel, Level 3, 7 Raffles Boulevard, Marina Square. MRT: City Hall. 6333 1788. www.rangmahal.com.sg.*

Stylishly executed regional Indian cuisine. Favourites are lamb shanks simmered in a saffron and cardamom flavoured cashew gravy laced with roasted almonds, and puffy *phulka* breads (a type of chapatti) that are freshly prepared table-side. **Indian**.

### $$$ Summer Pavilion

*Ritz-Carlton Millenia Hotel, 7 Raffles Avenue. MRT: City Hall. 6337 8888. www.ritzcarlton.com.*

Flanked by a pretty garden, the Summer Pavilion is famed for its dim sum specialities and subtle Cantonese dishes. Try the braised shark's fin soup studded with crabmeat and crab roe. **Chinese**.

### $$$$ Hai Tien Lo

*37th Floor, Pan Pacific Hotel, 7 Raffles Boulevard. MRT: City Hall. 6826 8240. www.panpacific.com/singapore. Brunch Buffet: 11.30am–2pm (weekends and holidays).*

Ascend to the 37th floor to luxuriate in exquisitely prepared Cantonese cuisine. Along with such signature dishes as soft shell crab, baked cod or pan-fried foie gras with scallops, you'll enjoy spectacular views of the city. **Chinese**.

## West Quays

### $$ Bon Goût

*60 Robertson Quay, #01–01 The Quayside. 6732 5234. www.bongout-cafe.com.*

The walls are lined with Japanese anime books, magazines and comfy couches. Between reads, check out the little café to the side; it serves up a lip-smacking menu of comfort food including hearty Japanese curries, *tonkatsu* sets, and tasty bricks of tofu flavoured with soy sauce. **Japanese**.

## LITTLE INDIA AND KAMPONG GLAM

###  $ Banana Leaf Apolo

*56–58 Race Course Road. MRT: Little India. 6297 1595. www.thebanana leafapolo.com.*

Known for its spicy south Indian food, this always-crowded restaurant serves up mounds of rice, vegetables and pickles on banana leaves. Most diners come here for the tangy fish head curry. **Indian**.

### $ Golden Mile Food Centre

*505 Beach Road.*

Situated at the western end of Beach Road, this hawker centre is a popular haunt among residents and office workers. Bear with the heat and long queues, and order hot favourites like Hainanese chicken rice and fragrant *char kway teow* (fried rice noodles). **Hawker Centre**.

### $ HJH Maimunah

*11 Jalan Pisang. MRT: Bugis. 6291 3132.*

A modest eatery with a fierce following. The homey fare includes tender chunks of beef braised in a creamy coconut sauce, chicken curries and a multicoloured spread of puddings and cakes. **Malay**.

### $ Komala Vilas

*76–78 Serangoon Road. MRT: Little India. 6293 6980. www.komalavilas.com.sg.*

The regular crowds come for cheap vegetarian Indian fare. Fast-food-style meals are served downstairs, while restaurant-style seating is available upstairs. **Indian**.

### $ Pho Lan

*#01–01 Prinsep Place, 44A Prinsep Street. MRT: Dhoby Ghaut. 6835 9441. www.pholan.com.*

Cosy and casual, Pho Lan serves wholesome Vietnamese fare. The rice paper rolls and sugar cane wrapped with prawn paste nicely complement the more substantial noodle dishes. End the meal with a potent Vietnamese coffee. **Vietnamese**.

### $$ Alaturka

*16 Bussorah Street. MRT: Bugis. 6294 0304. www.alaturka.com.sg.*

This charming restaurant serves Turkish fare such as fluffy *pide* (the Turkish version of pizza) and *sütlaç*, a caramelised Turkish rice pudding. After your meal, relax with a strawberry flavoured *shisha*. **Turkish**.

### $$ Café Le Caire

*39 Arab Street. MRT: Bugis. 6292 0979. www.cafelecaire.com.*

With only wall fans, the ground floor can get a little muggy; the upstairs room is more comfortable, though less atmospheric. Share the mezze platter and *meshawi*, a combination of grilled meats and vegetables. **Middle Eastern**.

### $$ Jade of India

*01–01/05 Soho @ Farrer, 172 Race Course Rd. MRT: Farrer Park. 6341 7656. www.jadeofindia.com.*

Jade serves the little-known "Chinese-Indian" cuisine. On the menu are vegetable ***hakka*** noodles and crispy beancurd with chilli garlic sauce, as well as traditional north Indian fare. **Indian**.

### $$ Muthu's Curry

*138 Race Course Road. MRT: Little India or Farrer Park. 6392 1722. www.muthuscurry.com.*

Muthu's formerly drab setting has been jazzed up. The huge menu consists of north Indian favourites like butter chicken and mutton curry, but their signature dish is fish head curry. **Indian**.

### $$$ Man Fu Yuan

*InterContinental Singapore, 80 Middle Road. MRT: Bugis. 6825 1062. www.singapore.intercontinental.com.*

This restaurant serves excellent Cantonese-style dishes and delicate dim sum in an elegant and classic setting. Try the crisp sugar cane wrapped with minced scallops. **Chinese**.

## ORCHARD ROAD

### $ Caffe Beviamo

*#02–K1 Tanglin Mall, 163 Tanglin Road. 6738 7906.*

It's difficult to go wrong with the generously portioned sandwiches, antipasto or the heaped chicken and avocado salad toasted with almond flakes. The luscious sticky date pudding is a popular favourite. **Café**.

### $ Food Republic

*Wisma Atria Mall, 4th Floor, Orchard Road. MRT: Orchard.*

Locals and out-of-towners love this massive air-conditioned food court. Decked out to be reminiscent of hawkers of yesteryear, Food Republic has retro push-carts selling dim sum and drinks, along with eight small restaurants offering Thai, Japanese, Korean, Indian, dim sum and local delights. **Food Court**.

### $ Marmalade Pantry

*Palais Renaissance Mall, #B1–08/11, 390 Orchard Road. MRT: Orchard. 6734 2700. www.themarmaladepantry.com.*

Although the quality of the food can be uneven, the basement venue remains a great place for people watching and fabulous coconut cupcakes. Check out the steak sandwich and sundaes. Sunday brunch is popular with the island's well-heeled. **Café**.

### $ Pondok Jawa Timur

*#02-66 Far East Plaza Mall, 14 Scotts Road. MRT: Orchard. 6333 8785. www.pondokjawatimur.com.*

Tucked away at the back of a busy shopping centre, Pondok's east Javanese street food menu is decent and cheap. Dig into the curry chicken, fried fish in tart ***assam*** sauce and mounds of ***gado-gado*** (mixture of vegetables). **Indonesian**.

The Rice Table

## $ The Rice Table

*360 Orchard Road, #02–09/10 International Building. MRT: Orchard. 6835 3783. www.ricetable.com.sg.*

Dining here basically involves a never-ending full-blown *rijsttafel* buffet brought straight to the table. At lunch, pay S$17.88 for 14 dishes. At dinner, expect around 20 dishes, all for S$28.49 per person. **Indonesian**.

## $ Thai Express

*290 Orchard Road, #B1–45/46 The Paragon. MRT: Orchard. 6836 8417. www.thaiexpress.com.*

Touted as the world's largest chain of modern Thai restaurants, Thai Express has outlets strewn all over Asia, with 21 in Singapore alone. The contemporary and casual joint offers authentic Thai cuisine at reasonable prices. **Thai**.

## $$ Chatterbox

*Meritus Mandarin Singapore Hotel, 333 Orchard Road. MRT: Orchard. 6831 6288. www.mandarin-singapore.com.*

The Mandarin's iconic coffeehouse is justly famed for its silky chicken rice and delicious local fare. Recently, it relocated from the ground floor to the 38th/39th floor of the Grand Tower. The lobster *laksa* and *bak kut teh* (pork rib soup) are also recommended. **Asian**.

## $$ Crystal Jade Palace

*#04-19 Ngee Ann City Mall, 391 Orchard Road. MRT: Orchard. 6735 2388. www.crystaljade.com.*

The flagship of the Crystal Jade chain is always crowded with fans who adore its authentic Cantonese food. Its dim sum and crackingly good roast meats are favourites. Reservations are essential on weekends. **Chinese**.

## $$ Din Tai Fung

*290 Orchard Road, #B1–03 Paragon. MRT: Orchard. 6836 8336.*

The original Taipei flagship is regularly voted one of the world's best restaurants. The Singapore outlet is equally famed for its steamed pork dumplings (*xiao long bao*)—tiny rounds of pleated dough filled with minced pork and intensely flavoured stock. **Chinese**.

## $$ Imperial Treasure Nan Bei

*391 Orchard Road, #05–12 Ngee Ann City Mall. MRT: Orchard. 6738 1238.*

The crowds arrive early, making reservations essential on the weekend. The menu is dominated by Cantonese fare of roast pork and a scrumptious range of dim sum (think deep fried yam pastries, sautéed snake beans and steamed rice-flour rolls stuffed with prawns). **Chinese**.

### $$ Indian Grill

*#B1–01 Tanglin Shopping Centre, 19 Tanglin Rd. MRT: Orchard. 6235 2712. www.indiangrill.com.sg.*

Decked out with huge mirrors, gilt sconces, red wallpaper and gold walls, the dining room is a soothing backdrop for the northwestern Indian menu. The tandoori pomfret is succulent and crisp skinned, while the buttery, fluffy garlic naans and parathas are perfect for mopping up the delicious sauces. **Indian**.

### $$ Kazu Sumiyaki

*5 Koek Road, Cuppage Plaza, #04–05.MRT: Somerset. 6734 2492.*

The small, obscure eatery can be slightly claustrophobic, but the crowds aren't complaining. The grilled ***yakitori*** items here are outstanding, especially the chicken meat balls, asparagus wrapped with pork belly, and marbled Wagyu beef. **Japanese**.

### $$ Patara

*#03–14 Tanglin Mall, 163 Tanglin Road. 6737 0818. www.patara.com.sg.*

Patara's timber panelling, Thai decor and scent of lemongrass oil are reminiscent of a Thai eatery in downtown Bangkok. It is easy to be satisfied with dishes such as aubergine topped with crabmeat or cooked with fried basil, as well as ginger-infused glass noodles baked with prawns. **Thai**.

### $$ Shashlik

*#06–19 Far East Shopping Centre, 545 Orchard Road. MRT: Orchard. 6732 6401.*

Baked Alaska, Tournedo Rossini, borscht and chicken Kiev are just some of the old-school dishes still offered at this institution. Some of the waitstaff have been serving diners for more than 40 years. Theatrics are highlighted by table-side preparations of the ***shashliks*** (a type of Russian kebab) and flambéed desserts. **Russian/ Western**.

### $$ Soup Restaurant

*#02–01 DFS Scottswalk. 25 Scotts Road. MRT: Orchard. 6333 8033. www.souprestaurant.com.sg.*

There are several outlets around town, but this one—with a fabulously kitschy faux interior modelled after a traditional Chinese home—is hard to beat. Healthy meals include such choices as double-boiled ginseng soups and steamed chicken served with lettuce leaves and ginger/garlic sauce. **Chinese**.

### $$ Straits Kitchen

*Ground Floor, Grand Hyatt, 10 Scotts Road. MRT: Orchard. 6732 1234. www.singapore.grand.hyatt.com.*

The traditional hawker food court concept is given a dramatic face-lift with the ultra-contemporary Straits Kitchen. The mind-boggling spread includes everything from ***laksa***, satay, and chargrilled stingray to chicken rice, tandoori and a host of Peranakan desserts. **Local**.

### $$ Summer Palace

*The Regent Hotel, Level 3, 1 Cuscaden Road. 6725 3288. www.regenthotels.com/singapore.*

Opened in 1997, the Summer Palace is a stalwart of the Chinese culinary scene. Kick off a refined Cantonese meal with a fragrant pumpkin soup, followed by cubes of seared pepper steak and braised vegetables. The aromatic, perfectly oiled fried rice, speckled with seafood, is a masterclass in technique. **Chinese**.

### $$$ Club Chinois

*1 Tanglin Road, #02–18 Orchard Parade Hotel. MRT: Orchard. 6834 0660. www.clubchinois.com.sg.*

Since it opened ten years ago, the Tung Lok Group's first modern Chinese venture has maintained its avant garde reputation and strong presence in the island's fickle dining scene. Signatures include braised foie gras with crispy onion pancake and roasted marinated rack of lamb in lamb reduction, fresh chilli-mint chutney and braised aubergine. **Chinese**.

### $$$ Hua Ting

*Orchard Hotel Singapore, Second Floor, 442 Orchard Road. MRT: Orchard. 6739 6666. www.millenniumhotels.com.sg.*

Hua Ting's elegant interiors are as well known for Oriental artefacts as for Cantonese delicacies. Master chef Chan Kwok's creations include silver cod baked with honey, and braised Australian green lips abalone. **Chinese**.

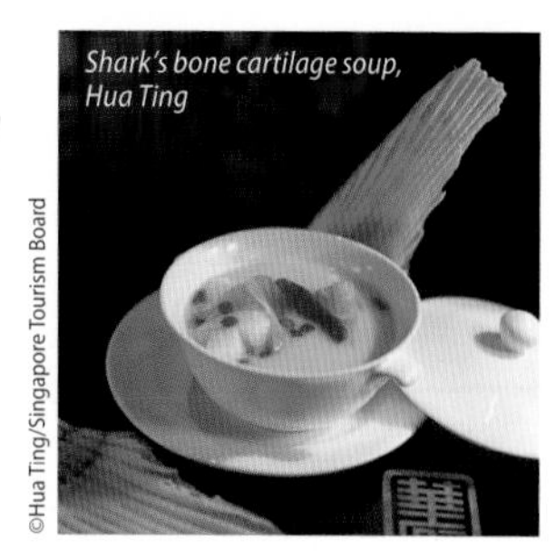

*Shark's bone cartilage soup, Hua Ting*

©Hua Ting/Singapore Tourism Board

### $$$ The Line

*Buffet Shangri-La Hotel, 22 Orange Grove Road. MRT: Orchard. 6213 4275. www.shangri-la.com.*

The ultra-modern space, just by the side of the Shangri-La's swimming pool area, was designed by Adam Tihany. There are 16 culinary styles to choose from, including a spectacular dessert spread with a 1m/3ft-tall chocolate fountain, ice cream ***teppanyaki*** and bread puddings. **International**.

### $$$ Mezza9

*Grand Hyatt Singapore Hotel, 10 Scotts Road. MRT: Orchard. 6732 1234. www.singapore.grand.hyatt.com.*

Mezza9 has nine unique dining venues under one roof, including a western grill and rotisserie, sushi and sashimi bar, ***yakitori*** grill, European deli, and a martini and cigar bar. The Sunday brunch with free-flow champagne is a must. **International**.

### $$$ One-Ninety

*Four Seasons Hotel, Lobby Level, 190 Orchard Boulevard. MRT: Orchard. 6831 7250. www.fourseasons.com/singapore.*

MUST EAT

Les Amis

©Les Amis/Singapore Tourism Board

To offer diners a greater variety of dishes to sample, One-Ninety recently unveiled a menu that features smaller tasting portions of its popular dishes. Look for items like applewood-grilled barramundi or grilled lamb loin with roasted garlic. **International**.

**$$$ Pine Court**

*Meritus Mandarin Hotel, 333 Orchard Road. MRT: Orchard. 6737 4411. www.mandarin-singapore.com.*

Pine Court sports a chic yet dramatic setting. The chef injects a modern twist into authentic Cantonese and Beijing dishes, and rustles up specialities such as Canadian sea perch steak with Japanese wine and honey. **Chinese**.

**$$$ Sage**

*No. 7 Mohamed Sultan Road. 6333 8726. www.sagerestaurants.com.sg.*

The intimate Sage is making headlines for its thoughtful Modern European menu created by owner-chef Jusman So. The pan-fried foie gras is excellent. **Modern European**.

**$$$ La Strada**

*1 Scotts Road, #02–10 Shaw Centre. MRT: Orchard. 6737 2622. www.lesamis.com.sg.*

After merging the former pizzeria and ristorante into one, La Strada has made certain that the spotlight still shines on its triumphant modern Italian menu and range of authentic wood-fired pizzas. **Modern Italian**.

 **$$$$ Les Amis**

*#02–16 Shaw Centre, 1 Scotts Road. MRT: Orchard. 6733 2225. www.lesamis.com.sg.*

Well-heeled diners populate this exquisite and recently renovated French restaurant. The cuisine is light and contemporary, with a focus on the natural flavours of the ingredients. The award-winning wine list of 2 000 labels is exemplary. **French**.

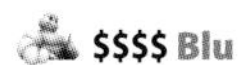 **$$$$ Blu**

*Shangri-La Hotel, 24th Floor, Tower Wing, 22 Orange Grove Road. 6213 4598. www.shangri-la.com.*

Blu offers a contemporary European menu with French inspirations. The stunning skyline, sexy lighting, soothing live jazz and designer decor all contribute to the restaurant's drawing card for the island's beau monde and expense accounts. **Modern European**.

**$$$$ Iggy's**

*The Regent Hotel, Third Floor, 1 Cuscaden Road. 6732 2234. www.iggys.com.sg.*

Iggy's is a regular on the world's best restaurants lists. The tasting menus boast the likes of homemade gnocchi with truffle salsa and ***sakura ebi*** cappellini with ***konbu*** and scampi oil. The intimate venue also has superb service. **Modern European**.

**$$$$ Jiang Nan Chun**

*Four Seasons Hotel, 190 Orchard Boulevard. MRT: Orchard. 6831 7220. www.fourseasons.com/singapore.*

Jiang Nan Chun makes a star turn with a brilliantly executed spread of Cantonese cuisine and top-drawer service. The dim sum menu is one of the best in town, and its week-end Oriental Brunch presents more than 100 delicious dishes. **Chinese**.

**$$$$ Nadaman**

*Shangri-La Hotel, Lobby Level, Tower Wing, 22 Orange Grove Road. MRT: Orchard. 6213 4571. www.shangri-la.com.*

Here, traditional Japanese cuisine, perfectly executed ***kaiseki*** and the smoky perfume of ***teppanyaki***, all come courtesy of chef Tomonori Kanemaru, who has been with the Nadaman chain for more than a decade now. **Japanese**.

## Scotts Road Area

 **$ Newton Food Centre**

*Corner of Clemenceau Avenue North and Newton Circus.*

Although some maintain that this iconic open-air hawker centre is touristy and pricey, it is still packed with diners especially in the evenings. Take your time to look around. Grilled stingray, deep-fried squid, and oyster omelettes are all-time favourites. **Hawker Centre**.

 **$$$ Li Bai**

*Sheraton Towers, 39 Scotts Road. MRT: Newton. 6839 5623.*

Named for the famous Tang Dynasty poet, Li Bai is a by-word for immaculate Cantonese cuisine served amid elegant decor and grand table settings of jade, silver and fine bone china. **Chinese**.

**$$$$ The Song of India**

*33 Scotts Road. MRT: Newton. 6836 0055. www.thesongofindia.com.*

Chef Milind Sovani's well-crafted and refined menu covers Keralan-spiced lamb shanks, tandoori prawns bathed in a pomegranate marinade and pan-seared ground lamb patties perfumed by cardamom, ground rose petals and raw papaya. The restaurant's setting is sophisticated and tastefully designed. **Indian**.

# HOTELS

Singapore boasts a wide range of accommodations for every budget and comfort level. The city's luxury high-end hotels are mainly concentrated along **Orchard Road**'s lively shopping belt, in the Marina Bay area, and at the fringe of the **Colonial District**, near the Central Business District (**CBD**). **Chinatown** hosts more intimate and distinctive boutique-style hotels like the New Majestic and The Scarlet, which are stylish and full of character. Other districts such as **Little India** and **Kampong Glam** offer value for money accommodations that are comfortable and tastefully furnished. Away from the city's bustle are Sentosa island's luxurious beach resorts. The service standard in Singapore is largely excellent, and well-trained hotel staff are mostly well-versed in English.

**Prices and Amenities**

The hotels and guest houses described here are classified according to the price for a **double room** for one night, not including taxes or surcharges. Since these prices often vary considerably throughout the year, you are strongly advised to enquire beforehand and to check the rates during the period chosen for your stay. Hotels accept major credit cards and offer air-conditioning unless otherwise indicated.

Many of the hotels featured in this guide also have first-class spas and restaurants *(see RESTAURANTS)*.

| | |
|---|---|
| **$** | <S$100 |
| **$$** | S$100 to 175 |
| **$$$** | S$175 to 250 |
| **$$$$** | S$250 to 350 |
| **$$$$$** | >S$350 |

**Online Booking** –

Rack rates (published rates) provided by hotels are usually higher than website deals. These rates are often attached with ++, which means you will pay an extra 10 percent service charge and 7 percent GST. Online booking is therefore often cheaper, with deals and promotional rates. To book a room, check the following:

**www.VisitSingapore.com**

The Singapore Tourism Board website has a hotel directory and an online booking service.

**www.StayinSingapore.com**

Singapore Hotel Association's website is a comprehensive Internet-based hotel reservation system managed by the Singapore Hotel Association and supported by the Singapore Tourism Board. It offers a wide choice of 21 000 rooms of different categories and rates from more than 50 hotels.

**Search Engines**

Alternatively, you can book hotel rooms while checking out the reviews from other travellers on the following websites:

- www.asiarooms.com
- www.asiatravel.com
- www.wotif.com
- www.hotels.com
- www.expedia.com
- www.ebookers.com

### Hotels on Maps

The hotels and guest houses are listed in this section under Singapore's major districts. On maps in the DISTRICTS section of this guide, hotels are numbered within a red house symbol; a corresponding Legend accompanies each map. Some hotels fall outside the perimeters of the maps in the Districts section, and may appear on the Singapore City map on the inside cover.

## CHINATOWN AND CBD

### Centre

#### Hotel 1929

**$$ 38 rooms**
*50 Keong Saik Road. 6347 1929. www.hotel1929.com. Smoking rooms available.*

After all these years, hotelier Peng Loh's debut boutique hotel in the heart of Chinatown is still looking good. The tiny lobby, stuffed with an eclectic connoisseur's collection of classic furniture, gives way to small, but comfortable and quirky bedrooms.

#### Royal Peacock

**$$ 76 rooms**
*55 Keong Saik Road. 6223 3522. www.royalpeacockhotel.com. Smoking rooms available.*

This hotel boasts ten beautifully restored shophouses equipped with modern luxuries. Charming touches include antique gilt-framed mirrors, plush purple carpets, and rich floral fabrics. The rooms are slightly small, but provide value for the money.

#### Furama City Centre Singapore

**$$$ 445 rooms**
*60 Eu Tong Sen Street. 6533 3888. www.furama.com. Smoking floors available.*

Centrally located in Chinatown and at the fringe of the CBD, the Furama is within easy access to shopping, food and entertainment venues. Tuck into an international (halal) buffet spread at **Tiffany Café & Restaurant**.

#### The Scarlet

**$$$ 80 rooms**
*33 Erskine Road. 6511 3333. www.thescarlethotel.com. Smoking rooms available.*

This boutique hotel is barely a step from the restaurants and bars at **Ann Siang Hill** and **Club Street**. With its gaudy decor (think gold wallpaper, crystal wall sconces, bright red lounges, and shimmering Bisazza-tiled ponds), the hotel looks like a set straight out of *Moulin Rouge*.

#### Berjaya Hotel

**$$$$$ 48 rooms**
*83 Duxton Road. 6227 7678. www.berjayaresorts.com. Non-smoking.*

Ensconced in a Straits-Chinese trading house, this was one of Singapore's first boutique hotels. Marked by a charming colonial-style interior and French windows, each room has its own distinctive character. The duplex suites come with quaint spiral staircases and garden suites have their own indoor gardens.

## Tanjong Pagar

### Amara Singapore Hotel

**$$$$ 380 rooms**
*165 Tanjong Pagar Road. 6879 2555. www.singapore.amarahotels.com. Smoking floors available.*

Recently refurbished, this business hotel boasts specially outfitted rooms and facilities equipped with the latest AV technology. Leisure-wise, dip into the Balinese-style resort pool, or feast at its popular **Silk Road** or **Thanying** restaurants.

### M Hotel

**$$$$ 413 rooms**
*81 Anson Road. 6224 1133. www.millenniumhotels.com.sg/mhotelsingapore. Smoking floors available.*

Located in the heart of the Financial District, the sleek M is ideal for business travellers. Rooms cleverly fuse a home and office vibe by offering a comfortable rest area and practical workstation complete with hi-tech accoutrements and broadband Internet access.

## Havelock Road Area

### Copthorne King's

**$$$ 314 rooms**
*403 Havelock Road. 6733 0011. www.copthornekings.com.sg. Smoking floors available.*

The four-star business hotel makes the most of its location with great views of the nearby river from its renovated rooms. It's also conveniently close to the Central Business District, Chinatown and **Zouk**, one of Singapore's hottest dance clubs.

### Furama Riverfront Singapore

**$$$ 605 rooms**
*405 Havelock Road. 6333 8898. www.furama.com/riverfront. Smoking floors available.*

This affordable four-star hotel is only a short walk from Chinatown and Clarke Quay. Ideal for business travellers, all rooms offer wireless broadband. Have an after-work drink at the **Waterfall Lounge**.

### Holiday Inn Atrium Singapore

**$$$ 504 rooms**
*317 Outram Road. 6733 0188. www.ichotelsgroup.com. Smoking rooms available.*

This 27-storey atrium-style hotel is dated, but scores for its strategic location at the intersection of Outram and Havelock Roads. Business travellers will appreciate the wired and wireless broadband Internet connectivity.
Its Cantonese restaurant, **Xin Cuisine**, is the place for delicious dim sum and fresh seafood.

### Grand Copthorne Waterfront

**$$$$ 574 rooms**
*392 Havelock Road. 6733 0880. www.grandcopthorne.com.sg. 17 non-smoking floors.*

Situated next to **Zouk**, Singapore's hottest dance club, this is one of the largest five-star conference/accommodation properties on the island. Rooms are contemporarily styled and equipped with business-oriented mod-cons. The hotel's new luxury accommodation "La Residenza", located on Levels 5 and 6, provides 24 high-ceilinged one- or two- bedroom units for long-staying visitors.

### Link

**$$$$ 299 rooms**
*50 Tiong Bahru Road. 6622 8585. www.linkhotel.com.sg. Non-smoking.*

Touted as the biggest boutique-style hotel in Singapore, Link is located in the heartlands of Tiong Bahru, surrounded by a smorgasbord of great, cheap local cuisine. The contemporary rooms come in three ethnic themes: Chinese, Indian and Malay.

## South Chinatown

### New Majestic Hotel

**$$$$ 30 rooms**
*31–37 Bukit Pasoh Road. 6511 4700. www.newmajestichotel.com. Smoking rooms available.*

*Lobby, New Majestic Hotel*

New Majestic Hotel

The stylish and eclectic New Majestic makes its mark with quirky, spacious rooms, each specially decorated by a local artist. Its rooftop pool has portholes embedded in the bottom through which swimmers can peek into the excellent in-house **Cantonese restaurant** below.

# COLONIAL DISTRICT

## Centre

### Strand

**$$ 132 rooms**
*25 Bencoolen Street. 6338 1866. www.strandhotel.com.sg. Breakfast included. Smoking rooms available.*

The Strand's budget rooms are surprisingly stylish and spacious. Besides deluxe rooms, there are "family rooms" that comfortably accommodate families of four to seven (per room), and "special rooms" with glass-walled bathrooms and distinctively vibrant furnishings.

### Carlton Hotel

**$$$ 630 rooms**
*76 Bras Basah Road. 6338 8333. www.carltonhotel.sg. Smoking rooms available.*

Conveniently located near the restaurants and boutiques at Raffles City, this recently renovated hotel offers rooms with views of the harbour and city. It also has a new extension of 159 stylishly designed Premier Rooms and Suites. Its **Wah Lok Cantonese Restaurant** boasts great dim sum.

### Fairmont

**$$$$$ 769 rooms**
*80 Bras Basah Road. 6339 7777. www.fairmont.com/singapore. Smoking floor available.*

The newly re-branded Fairmont offers luxurious guest rooms and suites with a sweep of contemporary amenities, excellent restaurants and bars. Its **Willow Stream Spa** is one of Asia's largest spa facilities.

###  The Fullerton Hotel

**$$$$$ 400 rooms**
*1 Fullerton Square. 6733 8388. www.fullertonhotel.com. Smoking floor available. All public areas are smoke-free zones.*

The former general post office and tax office in a gorgeous sprawling Palladian pile is now a deluxe hotel. Its location in the CBD coupled with stunning Marina Bay views make it perfect for business travellers. The pool and lounging area are especially delightful. The sleek **Post Bar** is great for after-work martinis.

### Hotel Grand Pacific

**$$$$ 237 rooms**
*101 Victoria Street. 6336 0811. www.hotelgrandpacific.com.sg. Smoking rooms available.*

The central location is a crowd pleaser. Kitted out with rosewood and leather furnishings, the refurbished rooms ooze a strong Asian influence. The Sun's Café offers a mix of local and western food. Though not a five-star hotel, the Grand Pacific (formerly the Allson) can command relatively high room rates, probably because of its location.

*Premier Room, Hotel Grand Pacific*

Hotel Grand Pacific

### InterContinental Singapore

**$$$$$ 403 rooms**
*80 Middle Rd. 6338 7600. www.singapore.intercontinental.com. Breakfast included. Smoking rooms available.*

Elegant and stately just about sum up the hotel's distinctive Peranakan-style interior. The rooms fuse Asian chic with all the standard modern conveniences. Its restaurants, **Man Fu Yuan**, **Olive Tree** and **Ko**, are impressive for the service and quality of the menus.

###  Raffles Hotel

**$$$$$ 103 suites**
*1 Beach Road. 6337 1886. http://singapore.raffles.com. Smoking rooms available.*

The Raffles still holds claim to being one of the most luxurious (and expensive) hotels in Singapore. The main draw is the building's stately elegance with its timber staircases, white-marbled corridors, Old-World finishings and a palpable sense of history.

###  Naumi

**$$$$$ 40 rooms**
*41 Seah Street. 6403 6000. www.naumihotel.com. Smoke-free except 2 patio suites.*

Naumi bills itself as Singapore's first luxury boutique business hotel. The extra-large rooms include in-room teleconference facilities, kitchenette and 50-inch plasma TV. Highlights include a rooftop infinity pool with great views of the skyscrapers, and a floor dedicated to female travellers.

Naumi Hotel

Naumi Hotel

## Istana Area

### Hangout @ Mt. Emily

**$ 6 dorms and 95 rooms**
*10 A Upper Wilkie Road. 6438 5588. www.hangouthotels.com. Non-smoking.*

With a "no frills, just fun" tagline, this hip accommodation for savvy budget travellers offers basic comforts like air-conditioning and ensuite bathrooms in its rooms. Clean, safe and cosy, it is a great place to meet other like-minded travellers.

## Marina Bay

### Pan Pacific Hotel

**$$$$ 778 rooms**
*7 Raffles Boulevard, Marina Square. 6336 8111. www.panpacific.com/singapore. Smoking only on balcony floors.*

The hotel's design weaves elegance with Oriental charm. It is the first hotel in Singapore to offer wi-fi automated mini-bars. Check out **Keyaki** for Japanese cuisine and **Rang Mahal** for innovative Indian fare. A bubble lift transports guests up to **Hai Tien Lo** for refined Cantonese cuisine.

### Conrad Centennial

**$$$$$ 507 rooms**
*2 Temasek Boulevard. 6334 8888. www.conradhotels.com/centennial. Smoking floors available.*

Conrad has a terrific location, right next to Suntec City and Millenia Walk. The contemporary interior is characterised by the use of lavish gold, muted brass, polished marble and warm rich woods, and adorned by an extensive collection of artworks by leading Asian artists.

### Marina Mandarin

**$$$$$ 575 rooms**
*6 Raffles Boulevard, Marina Square. 6845 1000. www.marina-mandarin.com.sg. 5 smoking floors available.*

Designed by John Portman, this hotel has one of the largest open atriums in Southeast Asia. Rooms afford views of the harbour and city skyline. The Executive Deluxe rooms come with flat-screen TVs, large work desks, ergonomic work chairs plus broadband access.

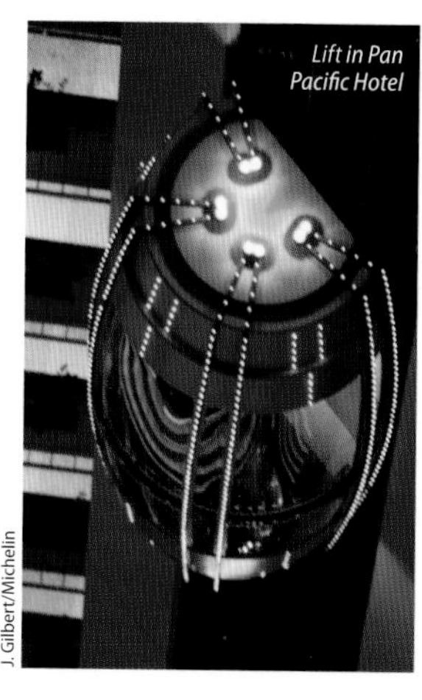
Lift in Pan Pacific Hotel

J. Gilbert/Michelin

### Mandarin Oriental

**$$$$$ 603 rooms**
*5 Raffles Avenue. 6338 0066. www.mandarinoriental.com/singapore. Smoking floors available.*

The refurbished and re-branded Mandarin Oriental remains a favourite with visiting celebrities and high-flyers. The classic John Portman interiors and Marina Bay views are dazzling, while dining options such as **Morton's of Chicago, The Steakhouse** and Cantonese restaurant **Cherry Garden** are top-notch.

### Ritz-Carlton Millenia

**$$$$$ 608 rooms**
*7 Raffles Avenue. 6337 8888. www.ritzcarlton.com. Smoking rooms available.*

The Ritz is justly famed for its plush rooms with luxurious bathrooms where polygonal windows frame magnificent views of the skyline. The public spaces feature a stunning 4 200 piece art collection that includes works by Frank Stella, Dale Chihuly and Henry Moore, all backed by flawless service.

## Robertson/Clarke Quays

### Gallery Hotel

**$$$ 223 rooms**
*1 Nanson Road. 6849 8686. www.galleryhotel.com.sg. Smoking levels available.*

Singapore's first "designer hotel" is located in the Robertson Quay and Mohamad Sultan entertainment district. Its art-centric inside features postmodern architecture, colourful interiors, and rooms with 24-hour free Internet access and satellite TV. Plunge into the glass-sided pool for underwater views of the city.

### Novotel Clarke Quay

**$$$ 401 rooms**
*177A River Valley Road. 6338 3333. www.novotel.com. Smoking floors available.*

The rooms of this recently renovated four-star hotel are clean and comfortable. Families will love the Family Rooms in which two children under the age of 16 can stay with their parents free. Buzzy Clarke Quay is just minutes away.

### Swissotel Merchant Court

**$$$$ 476 rooms**
*20 Merchant Road. 6337 2288/9993. www.singapore-merchantcourt.swissotel.com. Smoking rooms available.*

This business hotel is positioned by the Singapore river and near the CBD and Chinatown. Its three Business Executive floors house luxurious rooms and suites with upgraded amenities, including an Executive Lounge. The **Ellenborough Market Café** is wildly popular for its Peranakan specialties.

## LITTLE INDIA

### Broadway Hotel

**$ 66 rooms**
*195 Serangoon Road. 6292 4661. Non-smoking.*

The modest but comfortable Broadway is value for money, and perfectly located in the heart of Little India. Hop over to Mustafa

Centre for a shopping spree at any hour of the day or dine at one of the many excellent (and cheap) Indian restaurants along this stretch.

#### Albert Court

**$$ 215 rooms**
*180 Albert Street. 6339 3939. www.albertcourt.com.sg. Smoking rooms available.*

Old World charm blends with modern touches at Albert Court. Just a short walk to Little India, the hotel is located in a pre-war shophouse embellished with Peranakan carvings and motifs. The contemporary Courtyard Rooms provide broadband Internet access, cable TV and in-house movies.

## KAMPONG GLAM

####  Sleepy Sam's

**$ 59 rooms and 6 dorms**
*55 Bussorah Street. 9277 4988. www.sleepysams.com. Breakfast included. Non-smoking.*

This B&B for backpackers brims with character. Situated in the lively Arab Quarter, amid a row of traditional shophouses near Sultan Mosque, it offers free high-speed Internet access and a fully equipped kitchen. Some of the dorm rooms are designated for women only. The barbecue spot is a great place to mingle with other travellers.

#### Golden Landmark

**$$ 393 rooms**
*390 Victoria Street. 6297 2828. www.goldenlandmark.com.sg. Smoking floors available.*

Although it looks a little tired, the Landmark offers spacious, reasonably priced rooms with modern comforts such as broadband Internet access and cable TV. It is just minutes away from the vibrant Arab Street enclave and Sim Lim Square's IT haven.

#### Parkroyal on Beach Road

**$$$ 343 rooms**
*7 500 Beach Road. 6505 5666. www.parkroyalhotels.com. Smoking floors available.*

Located near Bugis, this hotel is ideal for business travellers whose offices are located in the vicinity. Book a table at the flagship **Si Chuan Dou Hua** restaurant, which serves authentic Sichuan cuisine, or try a traditional Indonesian or aromatherapy remedy at **St. Gregory Spa** *(see SPAS)*.

## ORCHARD ROAD

### Somerset MRT Area

#### Holiday Inn Park View

**$$$$ 344 rooms**
*11 Cavenagh Road. www.ichotelsgroup.com. Smoking floors available.*

Just off Orchard Road, next to the Starhub Centre, the Holiday Inn sits within walking distance of great shopping at Centrepoint and Japanese restaurants at Cuppage Plaza. The lobby is adorned with a dazzling chandelier, and the tastefully decorated rooms have views of lush greenery.

### Meritus Mandarin

**$$$$$ 1051 rooms**
*333 Orchard Road. 6235 7788.*
*www.mandarin-singapore.com.*
*Smoking floors available.*

The Mandarin once again sparkles after a recent multi-million dollar facelift. More changes are in the works. Its location, in the heart of Orchard Road, is unbeatable. The **Chatterbox** *(24hr Fri–Sat)*, famous for its award-winning chicken rice, is now on the 38th and 39th floors.

## Scotts Road Area

### The Elizabeth Hotel

**$$$ 256 rooms**
*24 Mount Elizabeth. 6738 1188.*
*www.theelizabeth.com.sg.*
*Smoking rooms available.*

Tucked away near the end of a cul-de-sac just off Orchard Road, the recently refurbished Elizabeth blends contemporary touches with European charm. It has the advantage of being mere minutes from the shopping strip, and yet being far away enough from the noise and traffic.

### Grand Hyatt

**$$$$ 663 rooms**
*10 Scotts Road. 6738 1234.*
*http://singapore.grand.hyatt.com.*
*Smoking floors available.*

The hotel's feng shui angled entrance has brought it perennial success, while soothing water features and acres of cool marble lure loyal guests back time and again. The Grand Wing rooms are particularly lavish with soft linens and Bang & Olufsen sound systems. Sunday champagne brunch at **Mezza9** is a must.

### Royal Plaza on Scotts

**$$$$ 511 rooms**
*25 Scotts Road. 6737 7966.*
*www.royalplaza.com.sg.*
*Breakfast included. Non-smoking.*

The first smoke-free business hotel in Singapore offers contemporary rooms with glass-walled bathrooms, generous work spaces and a free in-room mini-bar that's replenished daily.

###  Goodwood Park Hotel

**$$$$$ 233 rooms**
*22 Scotts Road. 6737 7411.*
*www.goodwoodparkhotel.com.*

This national landmark is sited on six hectares of landscaped gardens, with its Grand Tower designated as a National Monument. The grandeur of the hotel is still evident, and its original 1900 setting well restored. Guest rooms are tastefully appointed, while the dining options range from Szechuan to grilled steaks.

### Marriott

**$$$$$ 393 rooms**
*320 Orchard Road. 6735 5800.*
*www.singaporemarriott.com.*
*Smoking floors available.*

This landmark with its green-tiled pagoda recently underwent a much-needed interior refurbishment. Depending on room type, digital plug-in panels, Bulgari amenities and LCD TVs are offered.

### Sheraton Towers

**$$$$$ 412 rooms**
*39 Scotts Road. 6737 6888.*
*www.sheratonsingapore.com.*
*Smoking floors available.*

The Sheraton was the first hotel in Singapore to offer personalised butler service to all its residents. Besides the elegantly appointed guest rooms, there are six exclusive units of resort-style cabanas on the pool level.

## Tanglin/West End

### Orchard Parade Hotel

**$$$ 387 rooms**
*1 Tanglin Road. 6737 1133.*
*www.orchardparade.com.sg.*
*Smoking rooms available.*

Situated at the western end of the Orchard Road shopping belt, this Mediterranean-style hotel offers spacious rooms and plenty of great **dining** options from Japanese and Mexican to exquisite modern Chinese cuisine at **Club Chinois**.

*Deluxe Room, Orchard Parade Hotel*

Far East Hospitality

### Four Seasons

**$$$$$ 255 rooms**
*190 Orchard Boulevard. 6734 1110.*
*www.fourseasons.com/singapore.*
*Smoking floors available.*

It's everything you can expect from a Four Seasons: the rooms are plush and **dining** options exquisite. The rooftop swimming pool is picture perfect, and service unparalleled; the hotel has some of the most informed concierges in town. The elegant establishment is home to some 1 500 Asian and international **art pieces** displayed throughout the public areas and guest rooms.

### Orchard Hotel

**$$$$$ 653 rooms**
*442 Orchard Road. 6734 7766.*
*www.orchardhotel.com.sg.*
*Non-smoking.*

Although its lobby area has seen better days, the rooms are tastefully decorated and functional. The colour-themed suites are surprisingly very swanky and superbly designed. The award-winning Chinese restaurant **Hua Ting** serves consistently good Cantonese delicacies.

### The Regent

**$$$$$ 439 rooms**
*1 Cuscaden Road. 6733 8888.*
*www.regenthotels.com.*
*Smoking floors available.*

Built around a light-filled atrium, the hotel is decked out in luxurious furnishings and drips with glittering chandeliers. The 46 suites with private balconies feature an interior that reflects Southeast Asia's rich heritage.

The Sentosa Resort and Spa

Courtesy Singapore Tourism Board

### The Shangri-La

**$$$$$ 750 rooms**
*22 Orange Grove Road. 6737 3644. www.shangri-la.com. Smoking rooms available.*

Built in the days when a grand, opulent lobby was de rigueur, the "Shang" remains a favourite, much loved for its soaring lobby, swathed in acres of marble, and for its expansive, landscaped gardens. Aim for the newer and fresher Valley Wing's rooms.

## Bukit Timah Road Area

### The Metropolitan Y Hotel

**$$$ 92 rooms**
*60 Stevens Road. 6839 8333. www.mymca.org.sg. Breakfast included. Non smoking.*

The Y's rooms are tastefully furnished, clean and comfortable. Laundry services, self-service launderette and complimentary shuttle service to Orchard Road are available. For cheaper options, try the separate male and female dorms at S$45 (plus breakfast).

## SENTOSA ISLAND

### Rasa Sentosa Resort Singpore by Shangri-la

**$$$$ 459 rooms**
*101 Siloso Road. 6275 0100. www.shangri-la.com. Smoking rooms available.*

To date, Rasa Sentosa is Singapore's only beachfront property. The vibe is a little 1980s, but as a tropical holiday destination, that's not necessarily such a bad thing. Every room has a balcony with scenic sea or island views.

### Amara Sanctuary Resort Sentosa

**$$$$$ 121 rooms**
*1 Larkhill Road. 6825 3888. www.amarasanctuary.com. Non-smoking.*

This brand new resort set amid lush tropical jungle is an easy jaunt to Palawan Beach. The best rooms are the former British army bungalows and barracks that have been converted into romantic suites with outdoor Jacuzzis and rainshowers.

### The Sentosa Resort and Spa

**$$$$$ 215 rooms**
*2 Bukit Manis Road. 6275 0331. www.thesentosa.com. Mainly smoke-free rooms.*

The resort's stylish rooms were refurbished by celebrated designer Ed Tuttle. Bedrooms are spacious and appointed in contemporary furnishings and draperies. Sizable bathrooms sport wood floors, deep soaking tubs and vessel sinks. The spa's setting is a lush garden with a waterfall and mud pools. Enjoy a romantic dinner at the **Cliff,** where the grilled seafood is a winner.

### Resorts World Sentosa

*www.rwsentosa.com*

Home to six hotels with six different themes, Resorts World has its own Hard Rock Hotel, plus the plush Crocksford Tower, artistic Hotel Michael, vibrant Festive Hotel, family Equarius Hotel and honeymooners' Spa Villas.

## CHANGI AIRPORT

### Changi Village Hotel

**$$ 380 rooms**
*1 Netheravon Road. 6379 7111. www.changivillage.com.sg. Smoking rooms available.*

Just minutes away from Changi Airport, the hotel has spacious rooms that offer sea and garden views, complete with thoughtfully designed modern conveniences. To relax, head to the rooftop to soak in the **spa** or munch on a pizza at the terrace.

### Crowne Plaza Changi Airport

**$$$$ 347 rooms**
*75 Airport Boulevard #01–01. 6823 5300. www.ichotelsgroup.com. Smoking rooms available.*

With direct access to Changi's new Terminal 3, the Crowne feels more like a stylish urban resort than an airport hotel. Open walkways with greenery, sky gardens, water features and private resort-style access to rooms make this a welcome oasis for long layovers.

*Swimming Pool, Crowne Plaza Changi Airport*

# SINGAPORE



INDEX

INDEX

## S

**List of Maps**



**Photo Credits** (page Icons)

**Must Know**
©Blackred/iStockphoto.com *Star Attractions*: 6-11
©Luckynick/Dreamstime.com *Ideas and Tours*: 12-17
©Nigel Carse/iStockphoto.com *Calendar of Events*: 18-21
©Richard Cano/iStockphoto.com *Practical Information*: 22-33

**Must Sees**
©J. Gilbert/Michelin *Districts* 38-77

**Must Dos**
©Terraxplorer/iStockphoto.com *Museums:* 78-83
©J. Gilbert/Michelin *Parks, Gardens and Reserves:* 84-89
©Christopher Jones/iStockphoto.com *Outdoor Activities:* 90-93
©Michael Walker/iStockphoto.com *Kids:* 94-99
©Shannon Workman/Bigstockphoto.com *Performing Arts:* 100-103
©Alex Slobodkin/iStockphoto.com *Shopping:* 104-113
©Jill Chen/iStockphoto.com *Nightlife:* 114-121
©ImageDJ *Spas:* 122-123
©Marie-France Bélanger/iStockphoto.com *Restaurants:* 124-143
©Larry Roberg/iStockphoto.com *Hotels:* 144-155